Memoirs of a Clairvoyant

Unforeseen Circumstances

COLETTE BROWN

For Durga

INTRODUCTION

My parents said I was a miracle child. It was a miracle that I had made it and I was also the miracle that saved my mum's life. My mum had been very ill since she had discovered she was pregnant. Her blood pressure was deadly high and her blood tests showed something was very wrong. Her consultant advised her to terminate the pregnancy because she had three other children at home and he wasn't sure she could survive the pregnancy. My mum and dad didn't believe in abortion. They had already lost a child, my sister Isabelle, to leukaemia, when she was seven years old. They didn't want to lose another one. So they went ahead and I was delivered by emergency caesarean section two months early. I wasn't breathing so was rushed to be resuscitated. At the same time the surgeon saw that my mum's womb was covered in cancerous growths. He performed a radical hysterectomy and she was sent to intensive care. She was very ill indeed. My dad was left wondering if he would lose both his wife and his new daughter.

But I am here to write this book and my mum passed into spirit aged seventy-four in her own bed. The cancer never did spread. She lived to see her grandchildren be born. She told me if she had gone for the termination that the surgeon said they would never have spotted the uterine cancer and she wouldn't have lived very long. So she said that there had been two miracles that day. Yet, I know there were three: that day my spirit guide, White Storm, joined me on my life journey!

My parents gave me unconditional love and a happy childhood. I wouldn't call it a normal childhood: how could it be when I talked to spirits and warned of accidents in advance? This book is my story from

1

birth till now, age fifty-five. It is the memoirs of a clairvoyant. Most of what happened to me with regards to career and love was unforeseen by me. I seem to have spent a lot of my life saying, 'I never would have thought x or y would have happened to me,' but they did and I have been truly blessed. My 'unforeseen circumstances' have made me who I am today and it has been a roller-coaster ride! I hope you enjoy reading it as much as I have enjoyed living it!

1

I was born Colette Ferrie on the 21st of May 1961 in Bellshill Maternity in Lanarkshire, Scotland. I was a premature baby with ensuing problems: my nose hadn't developed properly, I had a problem with my palate and to make it worse I had a shock of bright ginger hair. Not strawberry blonde or auburn, carrot top red! I was born to Mary and Robert Ferrie and had two brothers, Robert and Joe, and a sister Kathleen. My other sister, Isabelle, had died before Robert was born and would have been twenty-two years older than me. My mum and dad were 'older' parents being forty and forty-two respectively when they had me. I was brought home to a council flat in Rutherglen where we stayed till I was five. I have memories of this flat even though I was young. I remember my mum and dad's silver wedding anniversary party when I was three where I marvelled at my brown shiny shoes with bows on them. I remember my pale blue dress and my dad counting my freckles on my arm. I remember my Uncle Joe falling into the anniversary cake after too much whiskey and I can almost feel the fabric of my mum's beautiful flocked dress. I felt proud of this glamorous woman with dark hair and hazel eyes flecked with gold. Yet I was like a miniature of my father with his red hair, pale skin and freckles, and bright blue eyes with long eyelashes.

I remember one evening feeling very afraid and upset but I couldn't understand why. I could see my mum in the kitchen making our tea while my brother and dad sat in the adjoining living room. I knew I wanted my Panda that my dad had bought for my Christmas but was too scared to go to my bedroom at the end of the hall to get him. I knew there was something bad in my room with him but all I could do was sit rigid with tears in my eyes while my dad once again called me his 'little soft heart'. I was close to tears a lot as a child and it became

3

his term of endearment for me. I was crying for my Panda yet I didn't want anyone to go to my room. My brother eventually went to retrieve Panda and all hell let loose. My mum had put on the two bar electric fire in my bedroom I shared with my sister. The council flats had ice on the inside of the window in winter and she wanted the room to be warm for us going to bed. My adored Panda had fallen off my bed and into the electric fire. His head had smouldered alight. There was thick smoke in the bedroom and in the hall. The fire brigade was called and we were all fine. I only felt relief once it was over. This was the first time I remember knowing something bad was going to happen and being paralysed with fear until the danger had passed. I was four years old. (A few weeks later my beloved Panda came back from the toy hospital with a huge orange crocheted square where his scalp should have been. Thank you Mum!)

Our flat backed onto the local primary school. On my first day my mum walked me down from the house, around the play park, and up to the school. My mum's best friend Mrs Doyle lived up the next close. Her son John was five days my senior and we played together. It was rumoured we had shared a pram as babies while our mums talked about life and shared apple pies from the Co-op. As a child, John and I both had individual holes in the fence through to the school. These holes had been put in place by numerous big brothers and sisters and previous neighbours. It was a swift duck under the fence at the back of the flats and straight onto the playground. John was a pal until we lost touch when I married at age twenty-one. Yet many years later and many miles away, he chapped my door while looking for someone else! Some friends are meant to be for life. When I was five we moved to a semi-detached house just a little bit down the road. It felt like heaven. We had our own front and back doors and a big garden with rose bushes and daffodils. I stayed there until I was sixteen. I visited it a few years ago and was upset to see it as it is now - a small and grey house with no flowers in a rather bedraggled area. Yet, back then, in the 1960s, it was a bustling, happy home, never without cousins or friends popping in. Yes, the kitchen units had Formica stuck to them to cheer them up a bit and the windows still had ice on the inside of them in winter, but, it was home.

I would say that this is the house where I have my first definitive memories of clairvoyance and mediumship. It was also the house I set on fire twice by accidentally leaving the frying pan on! Fire and me really don't get on! Or maybe it was just that I was an airy fairy child living in my 'own wee world' as my teachers would frequently tell my mum. Oh…I also had an 'amazing imagination'!

It was here that my little 'Nindian Boy' started to play with me regularly. I know now that he was my Spirit Guide who chose to stay close by me. I learned so much from him as a child. When all the kids played 'Cowboys and Indians' in the school playground I would always choose to be an Indian and was normally 'killed' by 'cowboy' friend, John. I preferred a bow and arrow to a toy gun. My little 'Nindian Boy' 'grew' up with me and is still here guiding me and connecting with clients during readings. More about him later!

I loved the new house but one thing really concerned me about it. The stairs from the hall to the bedrooms upstairs! You see, very soon after we arrived I noticed a strange feeling of being watched as I made my way up the stairs. There was a black outline at the bottom of the stairs and I forced myself to look straight forward while ascending them. A few days later I heard what sounded like an animal coming up the stairs behind me. It was snarling a bit and scared me. Every time I went up the stairs the animal would follow at my feet. I began to run up the stairs. My mum was always putting Elastoplast on my skinned knees and found it funny that most children fell down the stairs but I fell UP them. I couldn't tell her it was because a black beast chased me. That would only add to the other worries I gave her. One day when I was about eight years old, I had had enough. I was fed up of being scared every time I needed to go to my room. My dad was concerned for his wee 'soft heart' but I couldn't tell him about my fears as I had already freaked him out a few times. So I ran to the top of the stairs and then turned and confronted the animal. It was a black panther and she looked at me as if to say, 'Come on then…fight me!' I remember snarling at her with such rage that she sat down at my feet and never frightened me again. She did show up many times though and I felt protected by her and very loving towards her. It was only many years later when I heard of spirit animals, familiars and totem animals, that I realised that was what she was. She was never a pet. She brought me confidence in a world that could be quite frightening. She still prowls to this day. In fact, a client 'saw' her one time sitting at the side of the sofa. I do have some very psychic clients!

2

I was three when I had my first operation on my face. My nose was built up a bit and my palate was lowered a bit. My face was flat and moon-ish so the new contours were welcome. Unfortunately, I caught German measles which affected my eyesight and gave me a squint. It also took away about twenty percent of my hearing. (Years later it was found I had enough antibodies against German measles that my blood was taken every three months for pregnant woman who had been in contact with the disease and whose babies were at risk. Every cloud has a silver lining!) So as well as having a plaster over my 1960s style winged glasses and being hearing impaired, I had the original ginger curly hair and freckles. My mum and dad told me I was amazing and beautiful. They treated me like I was a princess. My mum was quite overprotective and I wasn't allowed a bike until I was eleven as she feared I would fall off and break my glasses or not hear traffic.

When I was nearly eleven my nose needed looked at again and I was honoured and lucky to become a patient of Dr Ian Jackson, the surgeon who rebuilt The Boy David's face. Beforehand though I had to have a gruelling year of my palate being stretched and lowered. I also had to have tubes in my nostrils to widen them. At one point my poor mother was attending with me the Ear, Nose and Throat clinic, The Eye Infirmary, The Dental Hospital and Canniesburn Burns Unit where the major plastic surgery was performed. Dr Ian Jackson introduced himself by asking me to 'pick my nose' and then having a laugh as we looked at different shaped noses on a chart. He explained that my earlobe skin would be used as nostrils and that there would be a kind of plastic at the front of my nose which would be sore if it got cold. He was a terrific man but the whole experience was painful and scary. I wonder now how my mum dealt with it. It wasn't until I had children of my own and had to attend hospitals with them that I understood how horrific it must have been for her.

I met a little girl at my pre-operation appointments. She had only part of her leg and was having skin grafts. We became friends but I always felt that she would go away and leave me crying. We were in hospital at the same time and as we played together I saw something that would trigger a deep seated fear in life. We were having a childish game of hide and seek the night before our operations. I ran into a room that I wasn't meant to go in and there, sitting up in bed, was a man with severe burns on his face. He had no nose but had some sort of feeding tube going into where it should have been. His eyes were stretched and barely open. He didn't have a mouth. I remember screaming and running out of his room terrified of the man without a face. The poor soul! What a thing to happen to him! Many years later I decided to confront my fear of masks. Any time I saw a kind of blank mask like a baseball mask or a Venetian mask I freaked out. It was only after deep meditation with a spiritual man that it was revealed that my fear of masks came from seeing the man with no face in the Burns Unit.

I had my operation and woke the next day with two black eyes and a very bashed nose. My friend had had her leg operation and was recovering. I felt strange saying goodbye to her and very sad. When I returned the following week the nurse told my mum that my wee friend had died as the cancer in her leg had spread and nothing could be done. In my heart I had known I wouldn't see her again. This would happen time and time again in my life. I never, ever got used to it.

I was back at school within a couple of weeks with my new nose and my lowered palate. My speech therapy hadn't been going well and I still had problems with certain words. ('Sausages' mainly!) The 'S' sound was a problem and I began to lose confidence in myself. No matter how much my dad told me I was pretty, I didn't feel it. I felt odd. The operations had mainly been done to help me breathe properly through my nose and fix my palate. (I still breathe mainly through my mouth.) My face didn't look so flat and I should have been happy. But I could see the small scars at the side of my nostrils and at the bridge of my nose. One of my hearing nerves had been damaged by an infection so I was a little more hearing impaired. My mum had cut my long curly hair as there had been an outbreak of lice in the school. I felt ugly and different. It was only a matter of time before a bully would go a step too far in teasing me.

Growing up in Blairbeth could be fraught with potential problems. There was the usual sectarian nonsense between my Catholic school, St Marks, and the Protestant School in Spittal. It never really amounted to much but there was an awareness of which 'side' you were on. There was also a hierarchy of boys and girls with John Doyle ranking with Elaine in the popularity/looks contest at number one, down to the ginger nuts like me and Gerry in the middle, to the bottom rung who had green snotty noses and/or skid marks on their pants. I was popular enough but not greatly. There was always someone who was better at something. My Highland dancing wasn't as good as Frances' Irish jigs. My singing wasn't as good as Bernadette's warbling. My spelling was atrocious so I was always picked last for spelling competitions. (Later on I found out I was dyslexic!) There was always someone better and if you were lucky, always someone worse than you.

There was one girl I remember. Let's call her Maryanne. She seemed to have it in for me for no reason I could fathom. She had lovely dark curly hair and a heart shaped face. One morning she told me she was going to fight me after school. The threats went on during the day and I knew if I didn't turn up that I would be bullied for the rest of my time at St Marks. I felt ill with nerves all day. Yet, as we met at the designated spot after school, I felt an odd sense of dislocation. I felt my panther was watching. As Maryanne poked at me for a reaction and taunted me about my glasses I realised that it was now or never. I was so angry. So instead of waiting for her to hurt me or humiliate me further I threw a punch and whacked her right on the nose. Blood burst out and she ran away howling. Friends and voyeurs ran away knowing the teacher would soon come. I walked home. I should have felt full of victory but I felt so sad. I had physically hurt her. I had her blood on my hand. I vowed there and then that I would never raise my hand to anyone again in anger. We both were brought in front of the headmaster the next day and both thoroughly belted for fighting. I felt ashamed. Yet Maryanne never bothered me after that.

3

There were a few psychic incidents from my childhood that have stayed with me in almost Technicolor. Some I can see as funny but others affected me more deeply. One of the funnier moments happened not long after we moved to the new house when I was five. My sister in spirit, Isabelle, had been around me for as long as I could remember but always only when she chose to come. However, in the new house we had two seats at the side of a long radiogram in the living room. I found that if I felt lonely, or wanted to chat, that if I sat in one of the chairs that she would come and sit in the other one. Yes…that's right…my dead sister who I never knew alive would come and we could play and talk. Our house had a kind of little hatch between the kitchen and the living room. It was very handy for passing dinner through on a Saturday night when we ate our tea while watching such choice offerings as Saturday Night at the London Palladium or The Val Doonican Show. We had the choice of three channels. Anyway, it was a Saturday morning I think and I had gone to talk and play with Isabelle by sitting on my seat. We chatted and laughed. She was so sweet. I remember looking up as I felt I was being watched. I could see my mum and dad peering through the hatch at me and the look of confusion and horror which was on their faces soon rendered me silent. I looked to Isabelle for support but she had disappeared. After that I wasn't encouraged to go sit on that chair again. As an adult I can see that my parents might have been really frightened but I can also see the funny side of it too. It was one of the first times that I felt that I should keep what I could see and hear to myself.

This was backed up when I was about ten and on a school trip to Culloden Moor where a great battle had taken place. My teacher ushered us all off the bus and immediately I knew we were all in danger. I could see the battle raging around us. I could smell fire and sweat and hear screams. There were women crying further away and bodies everywhere. And here we were all standing in the middle of it! I cried out to my teacher to get us away from the battle. She looked at me puzzled like I was winding her up. But I was slowly losing it, trying to drag my friends off the field. My teacher grabbed me and ushered me back to the coach while I watched open mouthed as the battle raged around my school friends. My teacher was angry. She shouted at me for upsetting the others and I shouted back at her and pointed to the battle, 'Do you not see it all?' and she replied, 'No Colette. I don't. It's only you that sees it. Now be quiet. What an imagination you have.' As I leaned back in my seat, sweating and tear stained, I realised that it was indeed only me who could see it and I resolved to be more careful in blurting things out in the future.

On the same field trip I had the indignity to fall into the River Spey. I was a strong swimmer even then and as the current whooshed me along I decided to swim for the bank. Yet I heard a voice in my head, deep and resounding, the way my guide speaks now, and it told me to go onto my back and float and for once in my life I did as I was told. A few minutes later I floated towards the bank and was fished out by my demented teacher. I believe now that had I tried to swim I would have become tired and drowned. (Many years later I was meditating on a tarot card and my guide showed me this escapade again and said it was a good way to interpret the card i.e. 'Go with the Flow!')

I don't remember ever being as scared of a spirit as I was of my first big premonition. I was so scared something bad was going to happen to my mum one night when I was about ten or eleven. My dad, my mum and me used to visit my brother Robert who lived in Cleland every few weeks to see his wee family and have some laughs. On the night in question I started to feel quite light headed and ill at the thought of our train journey home. We were going for the last train that night and I kept hanging back and telling my dad that we shouldn't get on the train. He told me not to be daft and that everything would be fine. But, you see, I simply knew it wouldn't be. As the train approached Cleland station I made one last attempt to stall us and nearly got myself a slap on the legs from my mum. Once we were on the train the intense feeling of anxiety didn't lessen and I put my head on the window and looked at my mum and prayed all would be ok. My dad kept glancing at me and occasionally shook his head. He simply didn't know what to make of me. I was shaking and sweating with anxiety. The closer we got to Cambuslang station the worse I became. The train was an old diesel type where you had to open the door yourself and each little compartment had a little door on each side of the train. When we arrived at our destination my dad stepped down. The train had stopped a bit further down the platform and there was quite a gap. My dad helped me down and I walked forward thinking how stupid I was and how much of a fuss I had caused. Yet when my mum stepped out of the train she missed her footing and slid down the gap between station and train. Her leg was hurt and my dad and the train guard had to pull her up. As she lay crying on the platform, the feeling of fear went away because, as I now know, the premonition had happened. There was nothing more to fear. She wasn't dead and her leg could be fixed. What couldn't be fixed was the look between my dad and me. He looked at me with real fear in his eyes as though I had devil horns and I looked at him with eyes that said, 'I told you so!' My mum's leg never really recovered from the accident. She went on to have two knee replacements in that leg.

One night not long after that, we were visiting my brother Joe and his wife in Leicester in England. They had had a baby, my wee niece Christie, and we had piled down to their small flat to see her. She was a little rosebud. I fell for her immediately. She still is one of the most important people in my life. On the last night we had gone out for fish and chips and had brought them back to the small kitchen at the far end of the hall. I had been sent up to the living room to fetch something and on the way back was stopped in my tracks by one of the fiercest spirits I have ever seen in my life. She was between me and my family and I stood still, frozen to the spot with fear. I could see them chatting and no one was taking any notice of me at first. The only way I can explain this spirit was she was very ghostly! She had long white hair and she wasn't solid. She swayed like the wind and seemed to hover. I could see my family through her. She looked at me with such malevolence that I thought I would faint and only disappeared when my dad shouted at me to stop standing in the hall and come get my chips. I dashed into the kitchen and told them I had seen a ghost. I think my brother's wife Sue believed me but the rest laughed it off, albeit nervously. Needless to say I didn't want my chips.

Later on that night the adults went to their bedrooms. I was to sleep on the sofa in the living room and I wasn't happy. I started to make a fuss but the look on my mum's face promised murder so I decided facing the ghost again was easier than upsetting my mum. (She was a Leo. She was ferocious when she needed to be.) I stayed awake as I was simply too terrified to sleep. The old lady spirit appeared again. This time she hovered over the sofa and seemed happy that I could see her. I was terrified but she indicated that she didn't want people in her house that were visitors that she hadn't invited. I remember saying in my head that we would be gone tomorrow. That seemed to satisfy her and she disappeared. I don't think I slept the rest of the night and was happy to be on the early morning train back to some kind of normality.

INTERLUDE

THE DIFFERENT WAYS I EXPERIENCED MY GIFT

When I was a child I was aware of seeing things, feeling things, predicting things and sensing and seeing spirits. It wasn't until later on in life that I realised these things had names and that I seemed to be open to many of them: clairvoyance, the seeing of things via the third eye, past present or future; clairaudience, the sense of psychic hearing that allowed me to hear sounds and voices that explained situations to me; clairsentience, the ability to simply feel things or know them. I also realised that I was mediumistic as I could connect and interact with spirits. I was an empath who simply picked up on what people were feeling or experiencing. I could see auras around people and objects. Mainly I just did what I did without questioning or labelling it. Yet it was good to pin things down when I started to teach Psychic Development and Tarot Studies.

People can have a very muddled understanding of the terms used to explain paranormal skills. I have always considered myself more clairvoyant than mediumistic even though I see my spirit guide and can have intensely accurate messages from spirit. I suppose I am quite a visual person so I really enjoy 'seeing' things and events and even how places used to be. So it surprised me that when people booked in for a reading with Colette Clairvoyant Tarot Consultant that they expected a, 'wee message from my Auntie Mary, who always comes through to me at the spiritualist church!' Sometimes I could have worked for over an hour with my Tarot and Guide helping them sort out convoluted problems only to be berated at the end because I hadn't delivered any spirit messages. But you see I only receive spirit messages if they seem really relevant and precise and these seem to burst through when a person actually isn't expecting them. I have spoken out in the past about how upset I get when so called mediums give very vague messages, for example, 'I have a lady here for someone at the left of the hall who may be a mother or a grandmother and she has glasses and grey hair'. Really? That's mediumship? No! Here is an example of true mediumship - I had a lovely medium called Max visit my psychic forum in Hamilton one Friday night. He knew of my scepticism but I had heard great things about him and already respected him. He came over to me and said, 'I have a message from your mum and she is laughing. She isn't giving me her name as she knows you think it is too common a name for proof so she is saying that her *three* knees are fine.' My jaw fell open and I thanked Max for a wonderful message. You see my mum was 'Mary' and I feel most people have a 'Mary' in spirit as it is a common name. But my mum had had two knee replacements in life and then the first one on the left knee failed and it was replaced again: she had three knees replaced! And her message was her wee joke to let me know that it was her! Now that *is* mediumship and it can be few and far between, not because there aren't great mediums out there but simply because the spirit world isn't simply living for us. They have their own lives and things to do and achieve on their spirit journey. Plus, I learned from my own dad that to break through from Spirit is tiring and not simple in any way. Spirits don't do it unless there is a good reason to do it. My dad took two and a half years to make his way back from spirit. In all that time I had no messages and only rarely had felt him around me. I had been worried that I had done something wrong. For two years before he passed I had been doing tarot readings at night and I never told him. He used to say that the tarot was the devil's tool and he was wary of paranormal things. One day I was ironing and was almost zoning out when my dad appeared. He looked at me with delight as though I 'finally did it' then vanished! A few months later he managed to come through again. He said it had taken him so long to navigate coming back because he had taken a long time to heal from all the strokes and frustration. He also told me that, 'You just need to be a good person to be where I am now.' This meant the world to me as I had turned my back on Catholicism and was about to start my journey into Shamanism.

I had two experiences of different types of psychic skills within a few weeks of one another that I feel explain clairvoyance and clairaudience very well. I had been working as a full time clairvoyant for a few years and still felt more skilled in clairvoyance than anything else. It was the one that I seemed to work with most. I had learned how to open and shut my third eye, exercise it and calm it, work with it and then rest it. I was reading for a woman whose husband seemed to be doing well at his job but would be moving soon. I saw him high up driving in a lorry and I felt he was on the road between East Kilbride and Rutherglen. To my third eye he appeared to be driving what looked like a big black and white cow! The woman laughed out loud as her husband drove the milk lorries for Robert Wiseman Dairies. These lorries had livery that was 'imitation cow'. We both had a laugh but I loved the way my third eye had given me his job and company even though I needed her help to place it.

A few weeks later I had a brilliant example of clairaudience or psychic hearing. It happened in a very similar way. I was reading for a woman and I wanted to talk to her about her husband's job. This time I didn't see anything at all but burst out laughing when, in my head, I heard the jingle, 'You can't get quicker than and Kwik Fit fitter, you can't get quicker than a Kwik Fit fitter...' I asked if he worked for Kwik Fit and she said, 'Oh my god, yes. How do you know that?' I was very honest and told her I had just heard the advertising jingle in my head. That is clairaudience.

My clairsentience seems to be about people but also about bigger things in society like a tsunami or earthquake. I can sense at times if something has gone wrong or is going to go wrong. This isn't like a clairvoyant prediction. It is more of a sore third eye headache and feelings of anxiety that only pass once the event has actually happened. So with this I don't see things or hear them, I just feel very out of sorts and very aware that bad news will come. I have never been a very anxious person so this can be relatively easy for me but trying to teach someone who has this gift but also has anxiety disorders the difference between the two can be very hard. Being clairsentient and having any mental health issues must be so hard. How do you know what is your premonition/psychic feeling/warning or what is simply your own anxiety? This must be confusing and very overwhelming at times. All I teach on this is bit by bit try to identify what you feel in anxiety moments e.g. where does it hit you? Is it your tummy? Does your heartbeat rocket? And then remember what your clairsentience feels like e.g. does it give you a headachy feeling? Or a sore chest? Then try to identify which is which but know that this may take time. Be kind to yourself.

Sometimes if someone is lying I can see it as a change of colour in their aura. It is like a flash of green-y grey. My daughters have always hated this skill whereas, as a mum, it has always delighted me! It doesn't always work because sometimes people are very good liars. It feels like it is a bit like a lie detector test: if someone is spontaneously lying it will pick up the energy change but if someone is a consummate liar who can make themselves believe their own lies, then I don't feel it works that well. Occasionally I will see red in a person's aura that alerts me to the possibility of danger but it can also mean anger. Many years ago when I had not long been in my Quarry Street premises in Hamilton I had a few phone calls from members of the public that asked if I felt anything bad for Princess Diana. This was interesting to me because a few days earlier I had seen a photo in the newspaper of Princess Diana on a jet-ski on holiday. She was having a ball and was obviously in love with Dodi Fayed. She looked as though she didn't have a care in the world. Yet her aura in her photo was scarlet red. This to me meant she was in danger and I hoped that she would not have an accident particularly on a jet-ski. Most people phoning me were unsure what it was that they felt but all expressed worry and fear for her. I certainly did not 'see' her death and neither did they but there was a general feeling of danger for her. A few days later Princess Diana was killed in Paris in a car crash.

I also had a terrible experience seeing red around a person and having such a bad feeling about them. This horrible feeling was indeed a prediction of death. In the 1980s there was a TV show called The Noel Edmunds Late Late Breakfast Show. It was Saturday night entertainment, a bit zany and very funny at times. Part of the show had peoples' names on a Whirly Wheel, like a wheel of fortune, and if the wheel stopped at them then they had to take a challenge before the following week's show. The challenges could be fun or adventurous. You just never knew until it was announced. Just before the wheel was spun I felt drawn to one name as it had red all around it. It was screaming danger at me and I knew instinctively that something bad would happen if this person was chosen. As the wheel spun I had a sinking feeling and said to my husband at the time, 'Please, please don't let it stop at his name.' It did. I felt sick. I felt dizzy and as they phoned him about his stunt, a bungee jump, I was yelling in my head, 'No! No!' I knew something bad would happen. What should I do? Could I phone Noel Edmunds? Could I tell them I didn't know why but it was important that this man did not do the stunt? I knew that no one would take me seriously. I wasn't even a full time clairvoyant then. I was a pharmacist. I felt ill with nerves but hoped I was wrong and tried to put it out of my head.

On the following Wednesday morning my radio alarm went off and the news came on. I heard that the man whose name had been outlined in red had done the bungee jump and the line had broken. He had died instantly. I threw up. I couldn't forgive myself for not having done something. I still haven't. It may not have changed a thing. Maybe it was his fate? But what if it could have been changed? What if other folk had acted on what their guts had told them? I am sure I wouldn't have been the only psychic to feel fear or danger about it. What if we all had phoned? I don't feel I will ever lose the guilt I felt then. I would phone, yell or be dragged kicking from the TV studio if it happened now. Sometimes this gift can feel like a curse.

4

I remember having what would have been described as my first shamanic experience when I was about eight years old. Shamanism is a spiritual path which connects you to the spirit in everything. All of creation has inherent spirit and this path allows you to connect and relate to all of the energies of life and nature. It is very nature orientated. Animals and plants are seen as great teachers. Intuition, magick and honouring of all creatures are basic principles. Everything has spirit or its own intrinsic energy.

We had a large back garden and I used to lie out on a summer's day on a blanket reading a book or magazine. It was a beautiful day. The sun was warm and the sky was azure blue. I remember feeling a bit drowsy and putting my book down. I felt drawn to the green of the grass. It was emerald and deep and full of a kind of happy energy. But then I felt drawn to just one blade of grass. My vision honed in on it and I was sure it was as good as welcoming me. Once I had looked at it for a few seconds it kind of vibrated and its green became greener. That's the only way I can explain it! What it was, became more. It was emanating 'grass' energy and I knew I wanted to experience that energy. But I didn't touch it. I just looked and before I knew it I had the most intense sensation of what *being* grass felt like and a deep sense of grass energy. Then I went from feeling what being that one blade of grass felt like to sensing the connection between it and all the other blades of grass in the garden…or maybe further. My mind couldn't really take it in. I wasn't frightened but I was rather shocked. I so wanted to run in and tell my mum that I *knew* what a blade of grass felt like…but after her reaction to the other 'shenanigans' I sadly decided that it was better to keep this one to myself. How would an eight year old explain this to an adult?

19

The next big experience I had was when I was thirteen or fourteen in the same back garden and probably on the same blanket. It was an intense experience but it didn't make sense at all until I was forty-two and met my soulmate, who would become my second husband. My dad worked hard and wasn't a great gardener and my mum had employed a gardener to cut our untamed back lawn. She was pleased that it was going to look good and neat like the neighbours' garden. I was lying on my blanket, reading, when this mad hippy appeared with an old fashioned lawnmower. I looked up at him and he smiled at me. My heart did some sort of mad flip and I tumbled into a sense of loving this person and needing him in my life. I felt so connected to him that I stopped breathing for a moment. He looked at me oddly and started his work. I looked back at my book and wondered what the hell was going on.

You see, this hippy was in his thirties i.e. very, very old! He was bald on top and had a long strawberry blonde ponytail at the back. I didn't see his eyes up close but I knew they were light blue, quite small and very twinkly. Although I didn't know how I knew that. He was so very skinny, wore blue jeans and had a black t-shirt on. His jacket which he had hung on the clothes pole was fringed. And I loved him! I really, really loved him. This wasn't like my love for David Cassidy or Hutch from Starsky and Hutch. Something stirred very deep in my soul. I glanced at him from time to time but I felt he was beginning to feel uncomfortable so I went into my room and tried to recover from my feelings. I was a teenager. He was an old man, in my eyes. He was so unlike what I would have been attracted to. He was bald for god's sake! But it wasn't about looks. I just knew I loved him somewhere in time.

The experience stayed with me and I wondered about it from time to time. I met my first husband, got married, had kids, got divorced... as you do! I had a couple of other partners who I loved for short times. Then one day, a friend I had met through a pagan group online introduced me to his old friend. And I knew. I just knew. I was forty-one and this man moved my heart. He was bald on top with a strawberry blonde ponytail at the back. He had small twinkly blue eyes and he wore jeans, a tee shirt and a fringed jacket! No! He wasn't my gardener from twenty-five years previous but he was so like him in looks that I instantly remembered the feeling I had when he walked into my garden. So you see… I think I had déjà vu in reverse. My future self had met and loved my second husband Jim but my teenage self felt something intense when she saw his doppelganger all those years before. I was feeling the love I have now, back then. It was in some way stimulated by a future memory! Confusing? Yes!

I had a wee boyfriend when I was fourteen. I was at an all-girls school, Elmwood, in Bothwell and we hung about with the boys from Holy Cross High on the train home. It was a mass of seething hormones but at least it was just for an hour a day. One day he said he had something to show me. In his room. But his parents couldn't know. I was naïve but very nosy so I went to his room. He shut the door tightly and we sat on the bed. He reached under his bed and brought out a deck of cards. He opened them and I had the strangest reaction. I felt I knew them but I was scared. The images flashed through my brain and felt it was too much for me. Again it was like a future memory. My first boyfriend had showed me his Tarot deck!

One of my circle of friends when I was at secondary school was a boy who was really sweet and had a head full of curls any girl would have paid good money for. He was such a lovely lad and I was so drawn to him. Yet part of me also felt I had to keep separate from him as I felt something odd around him. I knew that at some point he would be in danger and his family would be hurting for him. I could sometimes see a deep red colour around him. It felt like danger to me. So I kind of worshipped him from afar. A few years later I read in the newspaper that he had been killed while mountaineering. His family were devastated at the loss of their fine son. It was the same red colour I would see many years later around the photo of Princess Diana.

The other thing I remember about being at the girls' school was that I loved the convent house and the chapel that the nuns used. I used to go at lunchtime sometimes and just sit and absorb the calm of the place. I would watch the postulates deep in prayer and almost envy them. I knew even at that age that I wanted their serenity. I considered being a nun but put it out of my mind. I had found my passion and it wasn't Jesus. It was my Chemistry teacher! I had a crush on him for four years! How instrumental this crush was in me becoming a pharmacist I don't know but my Chemistry grades were always high and I really liked to impress him. I looked forward to Chemistry and even hung back in the morning to see him zoom in in his light blue metallic Ford Capri. He had a slight look of Martin Shaw as Doyle from the TV show The Professionals! Only slight, mind you, but it was enough.

My girls' school shut when I was in fourth year and we Elmwood girls were transferred to a new comprehensive, Cardinal Newman High, in Bellshill. Elmwood was small and so very pretty. I loved it there despite it never being warm and having a very scary headmistress in the form of Sister Mary Benedicta! I was good at English although I was dyslexic. I was just clever enough; I did well enough to be one of the girls and not well enough to be one of the geeks. Anyway, the day that Elmwood shut I stole the doorknob from the Chemistry lab that had been the daily meeting place for me and my beloved teacher. I don't know why I did it. (I tied all the teachers' cars together in the car park too with wool from the home economics department. I do love a good practical joke!) Years later I was running a psychic development circle in my premises in Hamilton and needed articles to test the students on Psychometry. This is the psychic skill where you use psychic touch to divine feelings, events or personal information from an object. The precious doorknob had become a paperweight and I grabbed it wondering if anyone would pick up anything from it. Most students got very little but one woman blew me away. She held it and her eyes lit up. She said she felt it represented love and had loving feelings associated with it. Correct! She said she felt it may have been from a hospital because she saw a man in a white coat. So close…my Chemistry teacher wore a white coat. She also smelled gas like from a Bunsen burner! Wow! That object had such strong energy and she was so good!

I was always interested in charity work and around my mid-teens a few of us got together to form Rutherglen Youth Action Group. We helped out at a disabled club called The High Hopes Club and I had many special times there. I had spent Saturdays when I was younger helping at a children's home working with Down Syndrome children. I liked to help. Through work with the action group I met the Queen and Prince Phillip. My mum was over the moon. I remember waiting to be presented to 'Queenie' and all I could think of was how very tiny she was. The following year myself and three friends formed a group to try to get an adapted mini bus for the High Hopes Club. The grant was from the Prince Charles Trust so we called ourselves Charlie's Angels to get his attention and to our amazement a few months later met Prince Charles and took delivery of our new community minibus complete with Charlie's Angels emblazoned all over it. My brother Robert was a commercial artist and he designed our logo which could look like crown or an angel depending on which way you looked at it. It was a happy time. My mum and dad were older parents and were nearly sixty years old. They gave me quite a bit of freedom to go places once they saw that I could take care of myself. I had met both Prince Charles and the Queen before I was seventeen! My parents were chuffed. I was gifted a holiday on a sailing boat called the Taikoo sailing around the Hebridean Isles as a reward for my charity work. This mad, intrinsically life threatening and life affirming journey became the basis for my interpretation of the Star card when I wrote my book 'Karma City: Weegie Tarot'. So much of my writing is based on things I have actually done and experienced. It has been quite a packed life!

5

I lied about my age to obtain a job the summer I left school. I felt I was old enough and wise enough to have a job in a hospital as I knew I wanted to work in one after I became a pharmacist. (Note to younger self- don't have preconceptions, retail pharmacy was always going to win!) I applied for an auxiliary nurse position at the Victoria Geriatric Unit when I had just turned seventeen. A slip of my pen made it look like I was eighteen which was the minimum age for the position. I felt rather grown up on my first day there in my blue uniform with my paper nurses' hat. The black lace up shoes didn't do anything for my legs but I wore them like a badge of honour. That first summer at the geriatric unit was amazing and gave me such an admiration for nurses. By the time I left in September I was exhausted with the shifts, emotionally done in and half a stone heavier due to calorific canteen food stuffed down in twenty minute breaks.

Yet I went back the next year. I forgot I had lied about my age and the same matron called me on it when she interviewed me again. For my sins she said if she gave me a job it would have to be a psycho-geriatric ward since I was obviously *so* mature. I said yes. By the end of that summer I had been scratched, punched, spat on and kicked. The patients who did these things were normally tiny little women who lulled you into a false sense of security before lashing out. It wasn't just me; all the nurses were abused in one way or another. Yet when the ward was quiet last thing at night and a good job had been done, all was forgotten until the next time. This was the place where I saw death most weeks and even at age eighteen I could sit with someone who had no relatives with them, hold their hand and simply be with them as they passed over. Never once did I see it as anything less than peaceful and normal at the end. Old women and men who were shrunken and debilitated in both body and mind looked calm and serene as the pure light energy filled the room and they took their last breaths which were normally just like every other breath. Then the nurses would wash the body and prepare it to be taken away in the big stainless steel box that clanged its way up the corridor of the ward. All the doors were shut so no patient would see it come and go. The nurses treated the body with dignity and care. The work of preparation was normally done in silence by two nurses who knew what to do and simply did it.

There were fun times as well. Nurses have a sense of humour that is in the gutter and that suited my Taurus nature just fine. The matron was terrifying and one night my ward was understaffed and there were three of us on for about thirty patients. The toileting buzzers were going off before the night shift came on and I couldn't run along the ward as it wasn't allowed by the matron. So I took a deep breath, took a dive at a commode and whooshed up the ward on it. It was like having a scooter. Unfortunately the matron had entered the ward at that moment. She shouted my name but I was so tired and done in that I simply turned and said, 'I know we're not allowed to run on the ward but no one said anything about riding a commode!" Matron's stony face cracked a little and she walked out the door before I could see her laugh. I knew I wouldn't be coming back after my second year summer. You need a vocation to be a nurse and I didn't have it. I wrongly felt that pharmacy would be easier and it was in some ways but not others.

I would say that the psycho-geriatric ward was the first time I saw collective group behaviour at a full moon. There were various jokes about how the moon made the patients agitated and some madder than they already were. Behaviour was worse and there was always a kind of heightened emotion. We had one wee lady who used to strip off and try to run down the stairs and make a break for the main road. She always ended up at the Victoria fountain at the top of the main Victoria hospital building. There she would be, sitting all pink and naked on the fountain, as two nurses arrived out of breath with a sheet to wrap her in and bring her back. She tried to escape every full moon and once this was known, the staff kept an eye on her. I used to feel spirits around me in the ward but never as much as at a full moon. I didn't like this because the ward was quite a sad place and some of the spirits were sad. Yet some of the spirit nurses were happy to be around and it showed that this place was a place that they loved and felt connected with. I often wondered if the Matron went back there after she passed. She was unmarried, had no children and lived for her job. This was her life and I am sure she loved it. The place ran well because of her and I will always remember the way her face cracked when she saw me riding the commode.

I was nearing the end of my first summer at the unit when I found out that I hadn't made the grade for Pharmacy and instead had been offered a place to study Pure and Applied Chemistry. This was frightening because I had focused so much on Pharmacy and my only other passion was writing and English but I had been told not to muddle my university application form by mixing science and the arts. My English teacher was stunned that I wasn't doing English literature and obviously felt let down. My English higher result was one of the top in the county. So I gulped and prepared to go and study Chemistry at university and maybe change to something else in second year. Two days before I was due to start a phone call came asking if I would come in for an interview with the professor of Pharmacology, Professor Bowman, as there had been someone drop out. I just knew that I could swing it. I prayed, lit candles and, without knowing it, did some mini rituals. I don't think I have ever presented myself so well since. I got the place and four years later had an Honours degree in Pharmacy (specialisation Pharmacology). A year after that I had my post-grad qualification and was a Member of the Pharmaceutical Society of Great Britain. A pharmacist!

The four years at Strathclyde University were intense, scary and opened me up to new horizons. I met my first husband on the first day of first year. I met friends of all cultures and religions and learned so much from them. I found my political edge and joined CND and protested against Israel's mistreatment of Palestine – thirty-five years later and this conflict is as sorrowful as ever. My studies were hard. I failed Pharmaceutical Chemistry every year and had to resit it. Yet I showed a very natural flair for Pharmacology and was able to specialise in this in my last year. I left with a respectable 2.2 Honours degree.

My last year as an undergraduate specialising was rough. I had to help research a drug for fertility and spent about seven months testing what it could do and what it couldn't. Seven years later this medicine was on the market as a nasal spray which forced ovulation in infertile women. I was over joyed to have been part of this. Many years later I learned natural fertility techniques from tribal women and fertility magick. My guide called me 'Medicine Woman Twice' which referred to my medical background and my 'medicine woman' background. I am proud to have had such a deep knowledge of fertility on both levels. I do regret the fact that some experiments were done on animals and fully expect to be reincarnated as a laboratory rat next life. The only way I got through it was that I believed that it was helping find new medicines and we only used what was necessary. It was a very small amount over the years. I know I would not have been able to do it now with my shamanic beliefs and my love of nature. I hated it back then but it was part of what we did. I don't really talk about it as I am ashamed. Yet it is a grey area because if my children needed a medicine that was tested on an animal to save their life then my principles and feelings would go down the toilet. Yes, I am spiritual but I am a mum and would do anything for my kids. Real life isn't so black and white.

I kept my guide at arm's length during my university years. I was a scientist you see and scientists don't have spirit guides! Or so I thought. My 'Nindian Boy' was growing up at the same rate as me it seemed and was a young man now. He was handsome and sometimes brash and sometimes funny. But I was fed up being seen as a bit dizzy and otherworldly. I needed to be more normal. Yet sometimes I would do palm readings for students. I couldn't read palms but I could pick up a lot just by holding their hands. Sometimes when I worked late at night in my lab I would sense the old professors and scholars whose energies still resonated in the old building. I never felt scared. I knew that my guide would be around me even if I wasn't exactly spending much time with him spiritually.

I worked for two summers and every Saturday in Boots the Chemists in Gordon Street in Glasgow. This was the Central Station branch. I had the title of Pharmacy Student and mainly worked in the dispensary and on the medicines counter. I loved it. It was close to the Albany hotel which was the one where most celebrities stayed when they visited. Most Saturdays involved celebrity spotting. I learned so much from my manager, Mr Colpitts, who was both funny and endearing. The only thing I didn't really like was going down to the stock room on my own. The stock room was in a big chamber under the station. It was like a dungeon and looked so at odds with the shelves full of shampoos and baby nappies. I was sure there was something unpleasant lurking in the depths. It gave me the shivers. I never waited long enough to actually see it. Most of the staff avoided the stock room whenever they could. Now I would love to go back and see what all my fear was about.

My pre-registration year was spent in R Gordon Drummond, in Bellshill, which I loved. Then it was on to the next stage of my career in pharmacy which lasted until 1996 when I gave it up to follow my dream of being a full time clairvoyant. Mad? Yes! Worth it? Oh yes! So very, very much!

6

I met my first husband on my first day of University. We started dating a month later, were engaged a year later and married in 1982! This probably wasn't what I had envisaged but I do feel that some things are simply meant to be. It wasn't an easy courtship as early on it was obvious that he had depressive qualities merged with a dependency on 'lad culture' e.g. rugby mates, golf mates, American football mates, drinking mates etc. I felt that given time I could help him, maybe even cure him of the depression, and this would lessen his dependency on the applause of shallow people. It took me nearly twenty-three years to realise that you can't cure someone's depression and you can't change someone who doesn't truly want to change. There were many good times and, especially near the end, such a lot of sadness and trauma. We had two beautiful daughters together who helped stick us together for a while but by 2001 I had truly had enough. I felt that every ounce of energy had been sucked out of me. There are photos of this time and I look at least ten years older than I was. I truly felt that if I didn't escape this marriage that I would die of stress and worry. Yet there was a huge amount of guilt at breaking my marriage vows and worry over how he would cope living without me and our daughters.

Yet on that happy day in 1982 I had no thoughts of failure. My first wedding photos show a very pretty young woman loving all the attention as a bride. My beloved Mum and Dad enjoyed the day along with a hundred other family and friends. One of my joys is that although it was a Catholic wedding, it was attended by my many friends of different faiths and none- there was a Hindu, a Sikh, a Muslim, a born again Christian, many Protestants and atheists. It was a great mix and simply a wonderful wedding. I couldn't have been happier as I set off on my honeymoon to Venice, a city that became my favourite in the world. My hen night had been amazing too, mainly due to the mix of pharmacy assistants who sure do know how to party. I had worked with Boots for a few years in the summer and Saturdays and most of the Weegie girls came to my hen night. This proved fun as my new Bellshill pharmacy chums were just as mad! My hen outfit was made out of things that came to hand in the chemists so you can imagine what it was like! My mum was horrified!

I started my first job as a fully qualified pharmacist the following July. I never once thought that I would give it up to be a clairvoyant. It was certainly an 'unforeseen circumstance'! Life has a way of surprising you! I worked hard, enjoyed dance classes to keep fit, visited my mum and dad and enjoyed my life. My 'Nindian Boy' was less available and months went by without me seeing him. This was fine by me as it was the mid-80s and I was more interested in climbing the career ladder, having my blonde streaks done and listening to Level 42. My ambition led to me being the pharmacist of the newly opened Shettleston Health Centre in 1984. This was a very stressful job but I thrived on it.

I was at the cinema one weekend with my husband and in the middle of the film I 'saw' a vision of my dad falling down in his living room. It was before mobile phones so I had to find one in the lobby and phoned my mum with fear. She looked in the living room to find my dad had fallen. When she got him up he was mixing up his words. I knew he had a stroke and rushed to take him to hospital. This was the first stroke. My lovely dad had nine more years of strokes that left him without speech and without mobility. He had always been a strong man with a beautiful singing voice. He was a great speaker, a socialist and a trade unionist. He believed so much in equality and wasn't afraid to stand up for his beliefs. I look back and see that this was when my belief in Catholicism started to die. My dad had been such a good person. He practiced his religion- mass, confession, benediction - every week. He hadn't done anything to deserve these horrific strokes. I remember a family member saying, 'Why him?'' and I replied without thinking, "Why not him?" This caused uproar. But you see, for the first time in my life I realised that bad things happen to good people. Being 'good' is not an insurance policy against strokes or cancer or accidents.

Life is chaotic and can change on a turn of The Wheel of Fortune. To think of it any other way at that time would have meant that God simply didn't give a toss about the people that honour him. I wasn't prepared to accept that. It seemed to me that there had to be a creator that we came from but after that life was a mixture of fate and freewill choices i.e. destiny. The rest was chaos.

I do feel that my dad's stroke set me off on a quest in some way to make sense of things. I believed in an afterlife- I had seen spirits since I was young. I had already studied many faiths in my teens but instinctively knew that something would come that would allow me to feel contented spiritually. Once I was in Ayr and I passed the window of a wee New Age shop. There was a tarot deck in the window that 'shouted' at me. That is the only way I can describe it. It shouted at me, got my attention and made me go inside to enquire about it. The man in the shop asked me if I knew the tarot and I said only a little. He said that I shouldn't buy that particular deck because it all was in Spanish. I sadly left the shop empty handed. But it shouted at me again! I looked at the visual of The Fool on the front and went back in and bought it-Tarot Balbi, my very first tarot deck. I can't explain how I felt. I couldn't wait to go home and handle this treasure! I felt excitement, joy and the feeling that I had met an old friend, one that had been with me in many lives and one that would always explain things to me. My love affair with the tarot started that day and has never become jaded or disappointing. I think in tarot. I speak in tarot. Tarot has been one of the main loves of my life and I still relish shuffling my deck to see how I can help people and how I can be the best me! I found it interesting too that when doing a family tree, I found that part of my heritage was Black Irish. This came from the time that some of the Spanish Armada was shipwrecked off the West Coast of Ireland and the sailors integrated into the community giving the dark swarthy looks of the Spanish! So my Spanish tarot deck was always meant to be.

It wasn't long after this that I had a reading with an astrologer and psychic called Leandra. He worked in a flat in Rutherglen. I had moved back and now lived five minutes from my mum and dad in an old house that I feel stimulated many of my visions and dreams. Leandra handled his tarot cards with ease. I had come seeking guidance because my husband's behaviour was impacting on me. He had a seasonal depression where he was full of beans in the summer and low and depressed in the winter. It looked likely that he would lose his job due to time off sick and his attitude. I was in despair because I loved him and so wanted to make my marriage work. I wanted a baby at some point but the house was expensive and very old. Every month presented a new problem with it and years later I saw a movie with Tom Hanks called The Money Pit and felt they had written it about our house. Leandra was caring but blunt. He said I would have two husbands in my life and both would be astrological fire signs. My husband was Aries and I laughed and said if I ever married twice it wouldn't be to another fire sign! (My second husband is a Leo- a fire sign!) I also said to Leandra that he was wrong; that he was simply seeing that I had two husbands in the same body. One who was pleasant and happy in the summer but was angry and sad in the winter of each year. Basically Dr Jekyll and Mr Hyde depending on the season. He looked at me sadly and simply repeated that I would have two fire sign husbands.

Leandra also told me that I had a clairvoyant gift and one day would do what he did. I laughed as I couldn't see how although I loved my tarot and the different spiritual path it was opening for me. I loved the Norse myths and legends and had accrued a Norse tarot deck. (This is out of print now but I still use it to this day. The designer kindly gave me one of his last decks!) My guide had begun appearing again when I was frightened of all the spiritual activity around me. Leandra was a help in showing me that I wasn't going mad and that I did have a talent. Many years later he would warn me about being 'a tall poppy' but that's another story. For now, my gift was finding a way to blossom but there were times when I was confused and felt I would be better off without it. I could access books and take advice from psychics but there was no internet back then and I felt very alone. My husband was as psychic as a brick but was reasonably supportive. I am sure he was scared sometimes. Yet my gift gave him reassurance soon after a family tragedy. It would also be significant in driving a wedge between us.

INTERLUDE

THE 'BOOT UP THE BACKSIDE' DREAM

I hadn't been very disciplined in writing these memoirs. In fact, I veered off to write a short eBook on love called Love Lessons: Find Love, Keep Love, Be Love. My creative side was also being fed by the success of my YouTube channel, Colette Clairvoyant. I found that I adored making my informative videos and sharing them with like-minded people. So my memoir file on my laptop hadn't been opened for a wee while. Then I had the following dream. It was so intense and very vivid.

The dream started with me walking round the small seaside town of Girvan where I used to holiday when I was a child with my mum and dad and sister. I loved Girvan. My dad was in his late forties and was the person who went swimming with me and let me drive the wee boats in the boating pond. I can still 'smell' the petrol from them that heralded in a special time with my dad as my seven year old self steered around the wee island and under the bridge. My mum would sit at the side of the boating pond enjoying the latest novel by Jessica Stirling or Barbara Taylor Bradford. Happy times!

In the dream I was the age I am now and was walking with my stick. I saw a gift shop and in the window there was a video that showed 'Old Girvan'. There was an old black and white photo on the front, taken in the 1960s, that showed fancy park gates. I bought it and tucked it under my arm and walked on. Dream 'Girvan' was like a mixture of Girvan and Blackpool or Southport; much bigger and more 'seaside-y'! I walked past pizzerias and chip shops and modern day pubs. Then I saw the park gates that were on the front of the video. As it was dreamland, they were stuck in between shops and pubs! I immediately felt drawn to them and passed through them. Then everything moved from being in colour to being in black and white! I looked around and all the deckchairs, windbreakers and ice cream vans were from the 1960s. The boating pond, the hole in the wall shop that sold chocolate pears, the Dr Who experience and the balloons and beach balls - all in black and white. I realised that this was indeed from the era when I had holidayed in the 1960s. I saw an old fashioned red telephone box - weird in black and white - and decided to phone my mum and dad and let them know where I was. I even remembered my old phone number 0141-634-2474! My mum answered and she looked to be in her late sixties and quite well and my dad was behind her. He hadn't had his stroke and looked about the same age and very well. They were in their wee flat in Rutherglen. They were in full colour. I told my mum that I was in old Girvan and everything was in black and white. She said, 'Oh how lovely.' And then my dad said, 'Why not look for us all there?' I heard his voice and even though I was in the dream I was so happy because after his first stroke he didn't speak well and here he was healthy and alive and speaking. I was overwhelmed. So I told him I would go look for us and mum said, 'Good luck darling. We love you.' I left that telephone box so happy to have seen them again. (Yes, I was in the box phoning them but could also see them answer and interact with me from a different time, even though they were now dead. Dreams can do that sort of thing!)

So I searched and searched every deck chair and in every café to find my wee 1960s family but we were nowhere to be seen. But I enjoyed revisiting the places in Girvan that I had enjoyed as a child. I began to feel very tired and sore - must have been medication time - so I decided to go have a coffee and a sit down. But before I got to the coffee shop I decided to visit an old art deco hotel. When I went in I was amazed because there were clocks everywhere. The entrance hall and the bar all had very old fashioned clocks - all still in black and white - but it was an intense black and white, more like a silver and charcoal effect. I looked at all the clocks and took my mobile phone out of my pocket and phoned my daughters. They were only a few years younger than now and were also in full colour. I showed them the clocks on the walls and in the lifts and even took them into the men's toilets where there were clocks on top of the urinals! I told them how they needed to know about how we had loads of clocks everywhere in the 60s and mobile phones had replaced them now. They were fascinated and I made a little video for them of the hotel and all the clocks. I remember feeling very proud of my children for their interest in the past.

Next I went into a coffee shop and ordered a coffee. I put my stick at my side and rested my poor legs. Suddenly there was a loud noise like an earthquake and cracks appeared in walls. The cracks had colour in them. Deep intense colours. I felt in danger. The deafening noise again and more cracks appeared, allowing colour to seep into the black and white. I hobbled out of the coffee shop and the ground was swelling up, cracking open and vibrant colour was starting to break through everywhere. I knew I had to get out of this old 'Girvan'. Two friends from the present time, Allan and Hazel, grabbed me and ran along the seafront and past the old phone box. All the time the colour was cracking through. I wanted to go back and let my mum and dad know I was leaving and say goodbye to them. Allan and Hazel yelled at me to keep going and dragged me through the park gates and I was left standing in full colour in Elderslie where they now live. The video I had bought had been left in old 'Girvan' as had my walking stick. I phoned my husband Jim to tell him I needed him to help me get home and that I had lost my stick. Then I awoke.

It was such an intense and interesting dream. I was delighted to have talked to my mum and dad but also devastated because I miss them so much. I know they are safe and well in spirit but I still miss them every day. I hurried about my day and resolved to think on my dream when I had time to meditate and be quiet. I took a number of things from it: in the dream I managed to be in a different time zone i.e. 1967. I got to connect with my mum and dad via old fashioned telephone circa 1986. I also connected to my daughters via mobile phone in about 2013. I was being urged by my parents i.e. the older generation to see if I could find us all. I also felt it was important to show my daughters i.e. the younger generation, important things from the past. Everything from the 1960s was in black and white whereas everything from the recent past and present was in vivid colour. And there were all the clocks! So I felt the importance of relating to the past maybe before it moved from black and white and was absorbed into the colour of everyday life. I could exist in the past only for a wee while before the colour of the present time broke though. I was not meant to stay in the past but I was meant to pass on knowledge of it. And maybe with all the clocks turning I had better get a move on! So here I am, back at my laptop, restarting the process of telling it like it was, knowing my memory of it could fade and the importance of another generation learning something from it. Yes, it certainly was a 'boot up the backside' kind of dream. Thank you, Spirit! And also a big thank you to Allan and Hazel for being good friends who rescued me from being stuck in the past.

7

The grey sandstone house in Rutherglen had been neglected but it was stunning. It had original fireplaces and cornicing and little nooks and crannies. It had the original bath screen, bath and sink. There was a stained glass window that splashed light down from the hall landing into the long entrance hall below. The garden was amazing and well established with apple trees and large hydrangeas. I leaned more towards a smaller, less expensive house but my husband loved this one and persuaded me that it would be better to aim high right away rather than do it gradually. We had good jobs and could just about afford the house. We didn't factor in the costs of repairs, fuel costs or rates. We were in our early twenties, both from working class families. No one could guide us and of course estate agents and lawyers were very helpful and persuaded us that we could have a mortgage. It was the 80s after all. The Harry Enfield character 'Loads a' Money' said it all. It was the time when it was good to be a yuppie. Looking back, I can see it was a big mistake. I should have stuck with my intuition and gone for the smaller, less expensive house. Yet, my husband adored it and I knew it would make him happy to live in a house like this. It was a very like one some of his friends lived in in the West End. Eventually the house became like an albatross round our necks. My husband lost his well-paid job and slowly the place began to disintegrate around us.

So why do I say that this house opened up my psychic awareness? Maybe this would have happened at this time in any house. Yet, the old house seemed full of spirits and stories and this piqued my interest. It also seemed to help me 'see' guides and events. So maybe we were meant to have the experience of it?

Almost from the moment we arrived I started to see a soldier standing at the foot of my bed. This soldier had terrified me in childhood and after a while had stopped visiting. This spirit showed himself in an army uniform but his face was all bloated and distorted. This was terrifying to me as a child but my mum always soothed me by saying I had had a bad dream. Now I was twenty-four and he was back with a vengeance. I would wake up screaming and trying to get away from him. Yet when I awakened he would still be standing silently at the foot of my bed. My husband had become used to my sleep walking and nightly murmurings but my screams at the soldier really irritated him after a while. Every time he visited I had full night terrors, screams and heart racing sweats. I knew there was only one thing for it; I would have to pluck up the courage to find out about my soldier. The direct route is best for a Taurus like me so the next time he appeared at the foot of my bed I swallowed my fear and asked him his name. I reckoned that in all his visits he had never once hurt me or approached me, so I would be safe. He told me he was 'Uncle John' and not to be frightened. In fact, he was one of my protectors for this life and watched over me. He said he never meant to frighten me and that his army uniform and bloated face would have explained who he was. I asked my mum about Uncle John the next day. She said that she had a brother John that the family never really talked about as he had been killed tragically while doing army manoeuvres in the River Clyde. When he was found his face and body were bloated and disfigured. After that Uncle John never worried me although he sometimes still gave me the odd fright.

I wakened up many nights trying to open a door half way up the stairs from the second landing. The problem was that in *this* house there was no door! My husband would waken me gently or I would waken myself. I would stand bewildered in tears looking at the blank wall. I knew that there should have been a door there. It was the door I went through when I was sad or scared. I was so confused. The next day I would soothe myself with music from my favourite band, Level 42. It helped me feel calm and more sure of myself. I seemed to 'visit' the room when I was particularly stressed or when life was getting me down but because I couldn't actually get through a door that wasn't there, it left me feeling worse the next day. Even when we moved house I still remembered the door that I could never get through. I knew someone lovely was behind the door. I loved whoever was behind the door. Then one night I had a dream. It went on for a very long time.

I remember standing on top of a hill looking over countryside towards a large white and grey house. I was walking with someone and I knew I was on the Isle of Wight. I have never visited the Isle of Wight in this life. I knew that this house was where I lived. Then I remember sitting on a chair in a hall eating an apple. It felt illicit as I knew I shouldn't have been there. I looked down at my chubby legs as I swung them back and forth. Then a maid came out with a broom and ordered me upstairs. She said I shouldn't be downstairs as proper folk were coming and they didn't want to see 'a Mongol'. She hit me with the broom and I ran upstairs past the first landing and up to the door I always searched for in my dreams. I banged on it, crying, and it was opened by my Granda who ushered me into the best place ever. It was a room that was cluttered with books and dust and a smell of tobacco. There were two big sofas in it and a chair. They were heavy chintz material. I ran to one and my Granda came and sat beside me. He gently whistled a tune and cuddled me. I was safe. I didn't know what a so called 'Mongol' was but I knew I was one and it was obviously bad and unworthy if I had been hit by a maid. Yet I felt safe and protected by my grandfather.

Once I saw this I realised that my attempts to enter the room in the old Rutherglen house were simply me replaying a past life. My own life was becoming more and more stressed and our house was old like the one in my regression. It also helped me understand why I have always been so connected to Down's' children. I helped out at a children's home when I was in my teens and had many Down's friends there. Sometimes I felt that I was going to have a Down's child of my own and felt sure that I would cope. This is because in the Isle of Wight, probably in Edwardian times, I was a Down's child myself.

Some time later I saw a documentary on the band Level 42 which I adored. The lead singer and world famous bassist Mark King said that he had a thing about a house on the Isle of Wight where he was born. He started as a milkman and admired the big house on the hill. He knew that if he ever made enough money that he would buy it, which he did a few years later. I saw him being interviewed in it. At that one moment I was taken back to being a wee Down's Syndrome boy looking at the house from outside. I felt instinctively that Mark King was living in *my* house. I have other past life stories but this was one of the first that convinced me that what we live and how we live is important to future lives.

The old house was great for parties and celebrations. We didn't have much money but I was creative and loved making my own Christmas decorations and cooking. We had two Cavalier King Charles Spaniels called Daniel and Donna who loved the big garden. We lived so close to my mum and dad that they could see our back garden from their flat window. This may sound intense but it was good because I was just around the corner after my dad had his first stroke. I remember my dad sitting in the hospital room bewildered as to why he wasn't getting out. He always called me 'his wee Precious'. On that day he said, 'What's wrong with me, my wee Perspex?' I looked at him and we both burst out laughing but I was crying inside. But the news was ok. He would recover. A few days later he came home and being close by felt wonderful. (Another reason maybe to have lived in this old house?) A few weeks later he was hit by a very big stroke which took away his voice and took away most of his mobility. He was in hospital and a recovery unit for three months. My mum and family were devastated. I felt as though my world had imploded. I still tried to get my dad to speak when he came home but he never regained his speech. He made a repetitive noise and could indicate yes or no but that was about it. Against what we had been told I continued to try to get him to say my mum's name because I knew how sad she was. One day I sat in front of him and said, 'Come on Dad, please try. Say 'Mary'. Say 'Mary', Dad. Please…Mary.' What happened next blew me away. My dad gave a look of concentration and pursed his lips and said, 'Hail Mary, full of grace, the Lord is with you,' and proceeded to say the whole 'Hail Mary' prayer. I was stunned. He couldn't speak but he could say a prayer. He was such a strong Catholic and I knew he loved the hymn 'Sweet Heart of Jesus' so I started it…and he joined in. My mum and I had tears streaming down our faces. We got to hear my Dad's voice again! I asked his consultant about it and he said that some things were so strong in your head that even a stroke didn't take them away. Thank goodness my dad wasn't a swearer! So every time I needed to hear my dad's voice I had to start him off with a prayer or a hymn.

40

There was more trauma to come while we lived in the old house. Through it all my gift was opening up so much that sometimes I felt very alone. I was still too angry and exhausted to actually ask White Storm, my guide, for help. Basically I was in my mid-twenties with a disabled mum, a stroke victim dad, a depressed husband and a job that some days required me to check 800 prescriptions! Something had to give and it was my health. I had the most awful attack of viral labyrinthitis. It took me off my feet for nearly three months. This was the first time that Spirit stepped in to call a halt to a workaholic, bloody minded Taurus who felt she could make everything in life okay. It wouldn't be the last time.

8

The big old house in Rutherglen continued to be both a delight and a stressful disaster. I loved the size of it and all the little odd old-fashioned things. It had a pantry area off the kitchen which was stone walled and had a low ceiling. This became a perfect place for my wee spaniel bitch Donna to have two litters of puppies! If you want the definition of cute, have a look at Cavalier King Charles Spaniel pups! They are adorable. The first litter had four strong pups and one very small one who we named Bianca as she was almost pure white. She didn't seem to be thriving and Donna had rejected her in favour of the stronger pups. My husband was away on some rugby or American football weekend so I did the feed every two hours myself. She didn't seem to be getting much better so the vet said I should get kitchen foil and wrap her in it and then put her in a sock and carry her in my bra to give her the body heat she needed. And still feed her by syringe every two hours. I didn't have kitchen foil but phoned my mum who lived around the corner and between her and her neighbours I got more kitchen foil than I could use that year. But it wasn't to be. On the Sunday night I fell asleep after doing feeds every two hours for two days. I wakened at five in the morning but wee Bianca didn't. She had passed. I cried my eyes out. My husband came home and buried her in the garden. I tried so hard to save her but it wasn't enough. She crossed the Rainbow Bridge that night but I will remember her forever.

My mum's friend and neighbour was Mrs Webster. She lived across the landing from us in the flat I lived in from age 16 to 21. She had also lived across the landing from my wee gran Isobel for many years along the road. So I knew her as both my gran's friend and also my mum's. She became very precious to me after my own gran passed. Her husband was called Peter and he had lost his legs due to vein problems caused by smoking. In the run up to my first wedding Peter was preparing a present for us. He had a hobby of painting and was very good in an old fashioned way. If I popped into the house there was mayhem as a painting was covered up. Our wedding present was amazing. It was a painting of a mountain in the Lake District of England and had pride of place in our first home. Peter was a man of few words but he expressed himself beautifully through his artwork. My honeymoon had been in Venice, a city that I love even more than Glasgow! I have visited it a few times in my life and never tire of the light and beauty of it all. We went to Venice again not long after Peter died. It was there that I had a glimpse of what Spirit life might be like.

We had arrived off the waterbus in front of the Doges Palace and I was walking towards the two obelisks that face into the lagoon. The crowds were milling about, the gondoliers were whistling and the heat rose from the ground. I caught my breath and stopped dead. In front of one of the obelisks was Peter! He raised his hand and waved at me. He had an easel in front of him and appeared to be painting the Doges Palace by the way he was facing. He looked very tanned and happy and he had both his legs! My husband looked at me as though 'what now?' and I told him. When I looked back Peter was gone. I knew I had seen his spirit but was baffled as to why I had seen it in Venice. I was happy for him though. What a stunning place to visit as a spirit.

When I next visited Gran Webster at her flat, I knew I would have to tell her but had no idea how she would take it. I simply explained to her exactly what I had seen. She smiled and had a wee cry. She told me that before Peter had joined the civil service as his main job, he had studied art in Venice and it was a place he loved with all his heart. This made me happy about my belief in the afterlife. I too adore Venice and would love to go there after I am done with this life, maybe to write a spirit book as I can't draw or paint to save myself. Isn't it lovely to know that something or somewhere that was precious to you in life can still be available to you in death? It is like your own personalised heaven!

I had been in the health centre pharmacy for two years and was beginning to be a bit bored with it. I often joked that if I saw another prescription for 'paracetamol tablets 500mg, two three times a day' I would commit hari-kari, as my Dad used to say. We had to pre-pack paracetamol, diazepam, nitrazepam and amoxicillin every day to cope with the amount of prescriptions for these medicines. The pharmacy ran like a well-oiled machine: three dispensers all dispensing and me at the end of the line labelling and checking. The workload was becoming overwhelming for one pharmacist though and the fun of building it up from scratch had gone. I am Gemini cusp and can become bored easily if not stimulated. It was time to move on. My next job moved me to Larkhall in Lanarkshire for a company called Scott Chemist. This started one of the happiest times in my pharmacy career. I stayed with Scott Chemist for eight years working in Parkhead Forge and the Olympia Centre in East Kilbride as well as the west end of Glasgow. I made many friends. I was back in retail pharmacy which I loved and had missed. The company allowed its pharmacists to bring in their own ideas and to be creative and rewarded them for hard work and dedication. I have such fond memories of Scott Chemist. I only left when they were sold to a national chain who didn't allow its staff to actually be part of it in any way. For example, it may seem like a simple thing but all the shops were laid out the same and two shelves were given over to water softeners and all their filters and chemicals. It was dead space as we lived in Scotland where the water is soft. No one listened. All was meant to be identical: one brand; one look. I felt like a robot. It was time to move on.

Luckily one of my area managers and friends from Scott Chemist had jumped ship earlier and invested in some shops of his own. I worked as a locum for a few weeks and then he asked me to job share with another old pal who had been a pharmacist with Scott Chemist too. I had my two children by then and it was dream. So it was onward and upwards to Milton Pharmacy in Giffnock and there I stayed until I walked away from pharmacy to become a self-employed clairvoyant. I enjoyed being a pharmacist. I still am a non-practicing one. But I never actually practiced again. Life had changed and I was no longer that woman.

Just before I moved from the health centre pharmacy we had a tragedy in my husband's family that affected him so badly that I don't feel he ever really recovered. He had a little niece called Helen who was a stunning wee thing, all blonde hair, big blue eyes and pouty mouth. She was a wee terror at times but funny and mischievous too. I had a kind of weird relationship with her. She made me laugh but at other times I found her too cheeky and sometimes didn't know whether I was allowed to say no to her. She was very different to my niece Claire who was very well behaved and slightly shy in company and I was used to children who did as they were told. I felt that Helen was cautious of me and I was cautious of her at times. My husband adored her and spent time with her when he could. One day my husband phoned me at work and said that Helen had been to the dentist and had a reaction to the anaesthetic and was very poorly in hospital. He was making his way there right away. She was eleven years old. Helen was on life support and was pronounced brain dead a few days later. The family imploded with grief. This wasn't helped by the fact that the Evening Times and The Daily Record picked up on the story and tried to get photographs of the bereaved family. Nothing would make it better. A mother and father had lost their child. A brother had lost his sister. Grandparents had lost their granddaughter. Aunties and uncles had lost their niece. But it became worse when rumours circulated that the dentist had been responsible for another child's death just a few years previous. The post mortem took over a week and many months later evidence showed that the adrenaline to restart the wee girl's heart that was kept in the dentist's emergency cabinet had been out of date. It was negligence. Helen was the second child killed by a dentist who never learned from the first time. I watched as the family struggled and I was present at one of the saddest funerals I have ever experienced. I had never seen such grief etched onto a father and mother's face. Grandparents and relatives looked like they had been stabbed through their hearts. I was heartbroken for them. My husband was heartbroken. I was sad but I was an 'in law' auntie to Helen so it would be wrong to claim this grief as my own. All I could do was try to help my husband and my mum-in-law whom I loved very much.

One thing did happen that my husband said helped him very much. One night, while Helen's body was still being held during the autopsy, she appeared at the foot of my bed. I sat up and nudged my husband to wake up as Helen was here. He sat bolt upright and I relayed what she said. She said that she was, 'here to talk to *him*. But he couldn't see her or hear her so I would *do*!' I found this funny. She was still a wee cheeky girl. Then she said to me, 'Tell him it didn't hurt.' And then she

45

disappeared. He had worried that she had died in pain; now he knew she hadn't.

Helen came back a few times and actually became quite protective of my children. She sometimes came with me when I went 'ghostbusting'. I believe she saved my younger daughter's life. Last time I saw her spirit she was a very elegant young woman still with blue eyes and icy blonde hair. She left me after I split with my first husband. This was right. She had always been his niece and her place was with him and his family.

Life went on. We were stressed about money and although I loved my job at Scott Chemist, I was exhausted. My dad and mum had moved to sheltered housing further away so I couldn't just pop round and see them. My husband's mental health was deteriorating. Our finances were regularly decimated by things like the chimney falling off the old house and the bay window needing fixed to the structure. Everything we earned was swallowed up by the house bills. Yet my husband still bought golf clubs and American football gear and went on tour with his team to the USA. I was happy if it allowed him to be happy but I had started to resent his depression and the things he did to make him feel better. Most of them involved him and a bunch of men drinking beer after kicking/hitting/carrying some sort of ball around some sort of field and all of it cost money we didn't have. I wondered if we really were suited and if we could continue on but I did love him and I was still committed to my wedding vows. Also I was becoming broody. I wanted a baby. He would have been happy to have children further down the line so it was kind of an abstract agreement that if it happened, it happened but not for a while. We had been together nearly 10 years and married for six. My 'happy accident' happened in December 1987 and was born the following September. My first daughter, Jennifer.

I had one of my most scary and sad psychic visions while I was carrying her. It made me promise myself that I would never, ever turn my back on my psychic gift. It was summer 1988. One of the hottest summers in history. I had been aware that my psychic visions had increased in clarity and intensity while I was pregnant. I now know this is a common happening. But I was truly worn out. I was hot, my blood pressure was through the roof and I wasn't sleeping well. When I did, I had dream after dream. One night I had enough. I said to White Storm, 'Please stop all this! I don't want it. I am going to be a mum. I have a good job and I want to be normal for a while. I don't think I am psychic anyway! It is all nonsense!' By the following morning I wished I had never said that. I told White Storm that I was happy to have this gift and would work with Spirit and my clairvoyance from then on if I just didn't have to see again what he showed me that night.

I had gone to bed early. I felt jittery and out of sorts. I raged at Spirit and said those words above. I fell asleep for a little while and awakened a few hours later. I sensed movement in the room and sat up. Then one by one the spirits of men who had passed walked in front of my vision. They were sad and some were angry. Some had yellow hard hats on. Others had safety vests. Some showed me they had drowned. Some showed me that they had burnt. The room ached with sadness and I cried and cried for these lost souls. How could some be burnt while others had drowned? Who were they? There were so many of them! I knew what I had seen came directly from spirit. I knew it was meant to teach me something. But all I could do was caress the baby in my belly and hope that whatever had happened would not affect us personally. I half slept and half cried most of the night. In the morning I switched on the television and the news was coming through that an oil rig in the North Sea, Piper Alpha, had exploded and was on fire. Many men had perished. Some had drowned, some had been burned. I had 'seen' them that night as it was happening. White Storm drew near and said gently, 'So…do you think you do not have the gift of 'seeing' now?' He looked at me and in one glance I knew that I was wrong to reject my gift and that the vision I had seen was given to me as a sharp shock to make me take it seriously. I knew I never wanted a shock like that again. It felt like I surrendered to my gift that night and I have never questioned it since. My heart went out to the men of Piper Alpha and their families. Tragedies happen but I just never wanted to see them in such detail ever again.

The night Jennifer was born was warm and stormy. As she came into the world there was thunder and lightning. Her dad joked that maybe she should be called Damian after the wee boy in the movie The Omen. We thought we were having a boy. She arrived distressed and was silent for a few minutes. They were the longest minutes of my life.

She had to have fluid suctioned out of her lungs. I sat up in the delivery bed praying and praying and when I heard her cry I just burst into tears. She was handed to me and all I can say was that I knew her. I just knew her. Her bright blue eyes seemed to say, 'Oh hello mum. I'm back.' She 'knew' me too. This feeling felt like many births; many past lives, each with a knowledge of one another. I knew she was part of my ancient lives and would be there too in future ones. The love of many lifetimes burst through me and I knew I would protect this little thing till my dying breath. That was probably why I didn't feel the 46 stitches the doctor used to repair the damage from the callipers that were used to drag her out of me!

I could only afford eleven weeks off work due to the house deteriorating and my husband having time off work. I loved that time. My dad held Jennifer in his one good arm and whispered words that made no sense and we all cried tears of relief that he had lived to see her. I was a natural mum. I used my instincts and they always served me well. It was a joyful time. Yet my marriage was not good. My husband was off work with depression and I felt that he would lose his job soon. I seemed to be juggling work and home and aging parents and caring for a man who didn't even seem to take joy in a little baby. He was medicated and very zombie like at times. He lost his job and I felt I was losing my mind. The house was falling down round about us. I had to make a decision that would surprise friends and family. My Taurus side kicked in and I simply knew we had to sell our big house, which had become a nightmare, and move to something that I could afford if my husband didn't work for a while. Within a few weeks we had a buyer and I had chosen a small terraced house in Cambuslang. My husband took little to do with it. In fact, I viewed the potential homes myself. I was taking a step back the way to secure our future. I would not allow us to go under. So we moved from a big semi-detached old home with loads of space to a two bedroomed modern home with a tiny garden and the living room and kitchen all in one space. It wasn't a great area but I felt relief. I knew I could make it work. I felt no shame in moving backwards to go forward. In fact, we had eleven years in that wee house. It was where my second daughter Jillian was born. It was affordable and I felt safe.

INTERLUDE

GHOSTBUSTING!

I was becoming known for my clairvoyant gift and interest in the paranormal by 1996. Over the next few years I would be asked to help people who thought they were haunted and I was happy to help. Even in the 80s, I had helped friends out who were scared of activity in their houses. Some were full blown spirits, others were poltergeists and some were simply a build-up of energy. Of course some were simply bad plumbing, loose roof tiles or something equally practical. I always looked for the practical answer first and ruled it out.

One of the first instances was when I was about twenty-six. My husband had a good friend and I became very friendly with his wife. We socialised and had good adventures together. They had a wee boy who was full of energy and had definitely been here before. They lived in a new estate in Bellshill. One day I received a call from my friend to ask if I could come over. She said that things were moving in the kitchen. I didn't have children yet and was able to zoom over and see what she was on about. I entered the house and felt such a mad energy and the toddler was acting up. I think he was hungry but my friend couldn't go into her kitchen. I went in and couldn't stop laughing as three packets of dried baby food on the counter moved back and forth for apparently no reason. I should have been afraid but it just struck me as mischievous and funny. I felt that the energy had moved upstairs so I went to the hallway and the bathroom door was open. The toothbrushes in the tooth mug were moving as well.

I felt so strongly that we had a little child who desperately needed to be given boundaries. So I yelled, 'Stop that now! That's naughty!' To my surprise a small boy spirit peaked around the banister and looked at me sullenly. He was dressed in modern clothes and had a full form. He was not unformed poltergeist energy. He truly was a small spirit. He kind of growled at me and disappeared. So I moved about the rooms upstairs until I sensed him in the baby's room. Then I told him that he shouldn't be here and that he was frightening the family. I again told him he was naughty to do this. I don't know where this approach came from, but it just seemed like the natural thing to do. He indicated that he liked playing with the baby so I told him he could as long as he didn't move things and that when one of his family came for him from the light, that he should take their hand and go with them. I told him that if he created any more mischief until that happened then I would make him go. He looked at me like a child would look at a teacher who had won the argument and agreed. I told my friend that there was a truce for now. Then I said some prayers to spirit and asked that the wee boy would be guided by his family to cross over to spirit. My friend felt the presence for another few days and then the place became quiet and nothing ever moved again.

My friend's baby was like a little beacon of spirit light. He was an old soul who would probably attract spirits during his life. I asked for protection for him and told his mum to connect with me if ever she needed me. A few months later the husband got a new job in England and our friendship didn't survive the move but I believe we all learned things from one another.

Sometimes I was called in by a spirit's family members. Sometimes it was by other 'sources'. I can't really say what or who the other sources are as I had been told many years ago that they would never confirm my connection with them, ever. I connected with these other sources at times in my career to help explain paranormal experiences or to help with certain situations. I stopped this work by 2001 when I was told I had no credit history when I tried to set up a new bank account when I left my first husband. The online adviser told me that I was either a ghost or a spy…I simply didn't exist. This terrified me so I simply said no if asked to help after that. Eventually I got my credit rating back: after the divorce it was so bad that I sometimes wished I had stayed 'non-existent'.

One night I was called to a flat in East Kilbride after the police had been to investigate a burglary: except nothing had been taken, some rooms had been wrecked but the burglar alarm showed no entry from outside. The police didn't know what to make of it. They had checked things out but had no conclusion. I remember I had just returned from my swimming class and was looking forward to watching LA Law when the phone rang. But this was too intriguing for me to say no to, so I quickly took my little ghost busting kit and headed towards the address. I had told the mum to take her baby and sit with a neighbour but asked the dad to be with me in case I needed help. The poor man looked terrified as the police had left and he had the possibility of a massive poltergeist in his house. To his credit he stayed and did everything I asked.

We opened the door to the flat and I walked in. I was very nervous. The man was scared out of his wits. The main activity was in the bathroom and the baby's room. The bathroom had plants knocked off the window which had fallen into the bath. There was a weird white powder splattered everywhere. The baby's room was a disaster. Little ornaments had been pushed off the windowsill and smashed into the floor. The lampshade was askew and it looked like some kind of mad wind had simply lifted things off their usual habitat. I always looked for the practical solution first but I admit, I was beginning to think that something intense was going on. The adult's bedroom, kitchen and living room were untouched. I checked the bathroom again and found no trace of activity or latent energy. I would have expected to feel something for the state it was in. I asked the dad to come into the baby's room where I felt an energy residue. I can't say he was delighted. I sensed some sort of energy behind the wardrobe which sat at a diagonal angle against the corner. It didn't quite feel paranormal but I knew 'it' was there. I indicated to the dad that he would need to move the wardrobe for me while I got ready to interact with the energy. I felt we were both building on one another's energy. I felt scared and uneasy and he was the colour of chalk.

So I stood with my incense and my 'spirit bag'. And slowly he moved the wardrobe. All at once something flew out at me and I screamed. The dad screamed and ran out the room. My heart was beating so hard. Then I focused on the 'ghost'. It was a little sparrow! I couldn't stop laughing and the dad came in and helped me catch it and put it out the window. All the mess, all the activity had been a little trapped bird who had come in the window that morning and had been trapped when the mum shut the window and went off to work. On investigating the white powder in the bathroom, it had come from a bottle of baby powder that had been knocked over by the terrified bird and had rolled behind the cistern. The poor thing must have been terrified, careering around the two rooms flying into ornaments and knocking them to the floor. It must also have been more terrified than me as it hid behind the wardrobe. Once again, the paranormal had shown itself to be very 'normal'.

Sometimes when I was called out, I would know immediately that there was simply nothing paranormal about an incident. Yet some people would be almost disappointed about that. I could never understand that mind-set. When I had been present at full blown scary hauntings people were genuinely terrified and relieved for the spirit to be moved on. Yet some people found it exciting to think they might have a problem spirit and didn't like being told that it was simply the pipes, the wind or worse, their angry teenager!

I visited a home one night that the family were simply very scared of what felt like very angry energy in the house. They felt they may have a malevolent spirit and were genuinely worried that the thumps and loud noises they felt might hurt them. I could feel the energy the minute I walked into the house and went straight to the epicentre of it, which was a teenage boy's room. The build-up of energy was so intense I felt a bit overwhelmed. I went down stairs to tell the family that the energy wasn't actually formed. It was a bit like poltergeist activity where energy becomes noisy and can move things. As I descended the stairs into the lounge I saw the teenager himself: a very mixed up, belligerent, confused adolescent who felt he had no control of anything in his life. I could see that he hated me on sight. Yet, I was able to talk with the family and open up discussion of adolescence and its confusions and while the family chatted I cleansed the room and asked for the energy to dissipate. This family were grateful for the advice and very soon the energies in the house were normal and the loud noises and bangs had gone. Success!

A few years later I would come across a mean spirit who made me less enthusiastic about ghostbusting when I was responsible for two young children and a depressed husband. I had already been called to a house on this particular street and had felt wary as I approached. The initial call had been about a haunting and had proved to be a poltergeist. This call was about a 'man' who had been seen and sensed. The family seemed to know who he was but I would never take that kind of info before I worked with a spirit. It was important to me to go in with a clean slate. They were obviously very scared. I had White Storm with me and also wee Helen, my niece who had died tragically years previously.

The room the spirit was in had been long abandoned by the family. I felt a very angry and vile spirit and as I opened myself up to talk to him I had reservations about how strong I was in the face of such a confused and unhappy energy. When the spirit manifested I held my ground. He indicated he had hung himself because life had got him down and people had never understood him. He was angry that he was being forgotten and that their lives were going on as before. I told him that he must leave and go to the light and his eyes glowed red with anger at me. The next thing I knew I felt that I was being strangled. His hands were around my neck and I was losing consciousness. It was very quick but I sensed my guides move in to protect me and I coughed and spluttered as he was forced away from me. I was so scared and felt quite broken but I used all my energy to shout at him to leave, to go away and to never bother this family again. I felt empowered by my guides and could feel his energy dissipating from the room. I used the last of my energy to cleanse the room and put protection up. I didn't even say much to the family who had heard the rumpus. I just said it was done and he wouldn't be back.

My husband used to say that I could go ghostbusting as long as I never brought anything home with me. That night I questioned whether or not I wanted to ever do this type of work again. I decided that I didn't. Yet two weeks later I had a call from another terrified family who lived two doors down from where I had banished the angry spirit. They had activity in an upstairs bedroom and were convinced it was a man who had hung himself. I felt so angry, not just at the spirit but at myself for not finishing the job properly. I had banished him from one home only for him to turn up a few doors away! I resolved that this would be the last time I tackled a negative spirit. I used my anger to fuel my courage and asked my guides for full protection. I also asked for the spirit's family members to come and guide him home, to the light. I knew this was best for him and also would allow me closure on a part of my life that I had enjoyed but had become just too intense. I went in like a warrior but was happy to see that the bad spirit had almost given up on his connection with earth. He was ready to stop fighting and go over to the light. It turned out to be a gentle enough night with tears from me when he went. I was happy for him and also happy not to have been strangled again!

And that was the end of my ghostbusting days. The lack of credit rating and my 'non-existence' helped me walk away too. I still saw spirits and passed on information from them and I still could identify if a building or home had an active spirit in it. I just never felt it was my place to get involved. I had done my stint at that office. I always had felt much stronger as a clairvoyant than as a medium and decided to be the very best clairvoyant I could be. I enjoyed predictions and helping people enhance their lives with my guidance with my tarot cards. I enjoyed simply seeing things for people and reporting in advance! I knew that there were many exceptional mediums who were aligned with spiritualist churches who were better suited to ghostbusting than me!

.

9

There was relief to be in a smaller more affordable home. It certainly felt like a goldfish bowl at times as there were homes across from us and behind us with just little lanes separating them. My husband had a new job and seemed to be handling it. I felt that it was time to have another baby. I fell pregnant quickly early 1992 and was very excited to be having a sibling for Jennifer. I felt very different from early on in this pregnancy though and felt strongly that I was carrying a boy. Work was stressful but enjoyable. I was traveling across Glasgow every day to my branch pharmacy in the West End. (This pharmacy would be the basis of one of my novels The Prescription many years later.) The fumes from the cars on the Kingston Bridge made me sick every morning. In the lead up to my first scan I had a little bleed. It wasn't much but I spotted every day after that. So a scan was arranged and I received the news that the baby's development was far behind what it should be. But there was a heartbeat and I hoped for the best. It was suggested that I should drop urine samples off every day on my way to work and have blood tests once a week. I felt very bloated very early on. My body seemed to be having a reaction to the pregnancy that wasn't right.

As the weeks went along the hormone that showed the development of the baby dropped. It was discovered that I had antibodies in my blood that were basically killing the baby. It seems that in my first delivery that my daughter's blood had leaked into mine and set up these antibodies. Since this baby had taken my husband and daughter's blood group, I was basically rejecting the baby. It was a time of great sadness for me but I felt sure that the baby could survive and I was prepared to look after him whatever his problems would be. So I continued the daily urine tests and weekly blood tests even though they were not offering much hope. Each afternoon I would phone the ward and ask for my results and most of the time I would be given not great news buffered with some caring words. One day I phoned for my results. I was on a break from checking medicines and my friend Janice was there helping out as a dispenser as my own dispenser was off ill. Thank goodness she was there. The voice I heard at the other side of the phone was huffy and almost annoyed at me asking for my results. She looked at them and said something I will remember for the rest of my life. She said 'the test results have now reached a level where the foetus is non-viable'. Non-viable!! I couldn't take it in. What did that mean? She answered that 'The foetus is non-viable. It is best if we book you in as soon as possible to remove the tissues'. Tissues?! My baby was non-viable and was now being called 'tissues'. I hung up and ran to the toilet to cry my eyes out. Janice sorted out the front shop and called my husband to come. I booked the next few days off. I don't know how I got through to the end of the day. Any prescriptions that day were checked about ten times each as my mind was so full of anguish, yet I had to work on.

The following day I was more in a fierce mood. I could not believe the words that had been used to explain that I was losing my baby. So I phoned the consultant and she explained that the baby really had no chance of making it to be born. I asked her if I could have a scan and she agreed. The scan was heart-breaking because it showed a very underdeveloped baby but you could still see that it was a baby. And it had a heartbeat!! I saw the consultant after it and she again suggested that I should come in right away. I told her that while my baby had a heartbeat, he was staying put inside me! She told me I was only delaying the inevitable and it was better for my own health if I didn't have so many antibodies in my system. Once again I told her that he wasn't going anywhere until he had died naturally. I had two more scans over 4 days. The second one didn't have a heartbeat. My baby had returned to spirit.

One of the saddest things was telling Jennifer, age four, that the baby in my tummy had died. She was devastated as she had been looking forward to being a big sister. Both sets of grandparents helped look after her while I went into hospital. This was a farce of a time. So many things were wrong about it. I nearly haemorrhaged when I was sent home. Three days later I had a phone call to say they had forgotten to give me my Rhesus injection to prevent loss of another baby. So not only did I have weird Anti Cw antibodies but my next baby may have died due to Rhesus disorder! My friend Janice came over with a bottle of Tia Maria and we had a night where I cried and sang and danced. It was almost like a tribal cleansing ritual. This was necessary because although my husband was so sad and distraught by losing our baby, he just didn't know how to articulate it in a supportive way. I know many men are like this and I feel some sort of counselling should have been available for us. But there was nothing.

Something amazing happened the night after I lost my baby. I was in bed and my Gran Isobel from spirit appeared at the bottom of my bed. She was holding a small baby and she said

'It's alright. I have him safe. I've called him Stuart.'

This was a surprise to me as I had called him Jack! But I was so overwhelmed to know he was safe that I just cried in thanks. It took years to find out why she had chosen the name Stuart. Basically, her family had a secret and a baby was given up for adoption. He had been called Stuart. My mum told me this years later before she died. Seeing my wonderful gran with my baby helped me immensely. I still see Stuart a lot. He is a mischievous, playful spirit who winds up his sisters at times and demands to be included in family occasions. At first I saw him as a baby, then as an older child. Many years later he showed up in a replica of his Dad's American football top. He was a young man with sandy hair and blue eyes. I know I will meet him properly when I go over to spirit myself.

Although the whole pregnancy and loss had been traumatic I didn't wait long before trying again. A few months later I was pregnant and full of worry as to whether I would lose this baby too. My antibody count was still high after the loss but early blood results showed that the antibody levels were growing. It looked likely that this child would not make it either. The new consultant told me that if I could get to 20 weeks they could give the baby a blood transfusion in the womb. The other option was that the baby could miraculously take my rare blood group and would thrive against the odds. I couldn't relax. I worried the whole way to about sixteen weeks as the antibody counts went up and down with no rhyme or reason. Then, they started to fall and kept falling!! This baby, they explained, must have taken my blood group and should be fine. And she was. In May 1993 my little Jillian Sarah was born after a horribly worrying labour. Yet as I approached the labour suite I was met by Alison, the same midwife who had delivered my Jennifer! White Storm's prediction all those years ago that both my children would be delivered by 'Alison' was true. Even at some scary moments, I knew she would be ok. We never bothered to check her blood group as we simply had been told many times that to survive she would have needed to have my blood group. Fast forward eighteen years later and Jill goes to donate blood for the first time. I say that it is a good thing to do as O Rh negative is the universal donor blood and is rare. She comes back with the stunning news that she is not O Rh Neg but has her dad's blood group. I nearly collapsed. How had this wee baby survived for nine months in my womb while my own body had antibodies against her? She truly was a wee miracle. There was no way she should have made it. But I know her big brother Stuart would have had something to do with it.

So I had Jennifer off to school and new baby, Jillian. My mum had to go in for a knee replacement a couple of months after Jill was born. This meant that my Dad, whose health had been deteriorating for nine years, had to go into a nursing home. This was so sad but my mum was determined to heal quickly and resume looking after him. However, the knee replacement didn't take well and she was left with limited mobility needing a Zimmer for in the house and a wheelchair outside. My dad kept expecting to come home but put a smile on when we visited. All we could say was that mum was trying to get stronger. Jill and Jennifer cheered my dad up when we visited. I was exhausted though. I had a new baby and a five-year-old. I was back at work three days a week and was doing the odd tarot party at night. My marriage wasn't great. I had asked my husband to have a vasectomy as I knew I didn't want any more children. I just couldn't face another loss plus to be honest I was so tired and looked like the walking dead. He said no. This was a shock as I knew that the vasectomy was an easier and safer operation than a female tube tying. He said that if we broke up he didn't want not to be able to have more children with someone else. Something died in me that day. Something died in my marriage. I felt that if he loved me enough then he would do this for me, for us. It also hit home that maybe he did realise that there was a chance we would separate after my many ultimatums. My wedding vows didn't seem quite as strong after that day.

In January of 1994 I did a tarot reading for my brother Joe who was up from England visiting my Mum and Dad. He was having problems at work and asked me to help. As I looked at the six months ahead for him I saw that, in three months' time, his dad would die. This then hit me that this was my dad too. I felt sick and full of sorrow and so conflicted. In all honesty I had prayed for the last couple of years that my poor Dad would be released from a life that had very little quality in it. He couldn't speak, had limited mobility and had all sorts of problems from his brain injury from the strokes. So part of me was happy that he would be able to leave his old, wasted body behind. I had no doubt he would go straight to heaven. He was just a good man who would have helped you in any way he could. He needed to go home to his Jesus and rest for a while. But I couldn't bear to lose him. After I lost my baby it was he who had held me tight in his one good arm and soothed me with nonsense words. He was my Dad and I had always adored him so I put the prediction out of my head. I called it rubbish and a mistake. I denied it in my own head. My mum continued to improve in hospital with daily physio and counselling as she wasn't dealing well with the guilt of not being able to take care of my Dad. Three months after the reading, to the day, my wonderful Dad died. It was less than two years since I had lost Stuart. I was thirty-three. Two things happened in the month that followed: I saw a divorce lawyer about how to get a divorce and I lost all faith in Catholicism. It simply had no meaning to me now my Dad was gone. I realised that his faith hadn't helped him in his later years to have any quality of life. He was a good man and his faith said that good, pious men would be cherished by his God. He wasn't and I was raging! I still believed in Jesus as a god but not in the way taught by the church, by dogma and by people who couldn't hold a torch to my dad. I believed in a creator who was known by many names and none. I also believed that only some things are fated, others are destiny choices and a lot is, well, just chaos. My dad was buried on Good Friday in the church he was married in as a young man. The church was packed because of the Good Friday Mass and it was so solemn that I thought I would go mad. I pushed my Mum in her wheelchair after the coffin as many eyes cried. Two years later, my Mum would be the one in the coffin.

We did have two good years with my Mum. Although she was devastated at the loss of her soul mate, she was also free of the guilt of not being able to look after him. She had her little sheltered house and I was there as often as I could be. She adored all her grandchildren. I feel she had a real soft spot for Jennifer who had eye problems and wore wee glasses and looked a bit like me as a child. Although Jill was young, both girls knew just to sit on her lap and she would read to them. They were gentle with her and it was a joy to see her with them. I never did go for the divorce at that time. My lovely mum- in- law explained to me that if I still wanted one in six months then she would be supportive of it but for now, she felt I was doing it because I had lost my Dad. It was for the wrong reasons and she asked me to delay a decision. She was right. If I had proceeded, then it would have simply been because I felt that no man could match up to my Dad so why bother being married at all? I also had no energy and was worried about my Mum.

My mum died in 1996. Both my Mum, my Dad and my sister Isabelle died in the month of March. It still is a hard month for me. The funeral day was so sad. The news came through on the way to the crematorium that a mad man had massacred children in a school in Dunblane. My Mum had loved children and always said, 'How could anyone be bad to a wee child?' I knew my Mum would be on her spirit journey but would be taking some time to send comfort to the parents who, like her, had lost a child. I hugged my own two close that night as most parents did I am sure. I just wanted to keep them safe and I also wanted life to be different. It was such a struggle. I had a good job three days a week in a nice pharmacy and enjoyed it but I enjoyed my tarot parties more. Jillian was not an easy child. She was clingy and anxious and I wanted to spend more time with her. I was fed up with childminders and nurseries and getting in after 7pm. I wanted to be there to take Jennifer to school and be there for her coming home. I wanted to be creative and help people in a way that suited my soul. My husband had been made redundant again but had a promise of another job in a few months; one that might be better suited to his temperament and would have a company car and reasonable salary. I had never really thought I would have the courage to walk away from pharmacy towards a hazy dream of being a full time clairvoyant. Yet, in three and a half years I had lost my baby, my dad and my mum. Something in my brain said 'now or never'. Life is too short not to be happy. I asked for some signs and I got them. In October 1996, I opened the doors to my first premises in Quarry Street Hamilton. I was thirty-five and was ready to live my life on my terms. If I failed, I could always go back to pharmacy. Yet I felt sure that something magickal would happen. That not only would I help people but that I would find myself spiritually while I was doing it. It was like opening a brand new book, with a brand new title and a brand new story.

INTERLUDE

MYSTIC CHALLENGE

By 1999 I had my own astrology slot on a weekly magazine show on my local TV station, Lanarkshire TV. It was good fun and my slots had gradually expanded from two five minute slots to two ten minute slots one at the start and one at the end of the hour long programme, 'to keep viewers tuned in.' I had been very nervous at the start but then had taken to it like a duck to water. I enjoyed the fact that we transmitted from an old asylum which was full of spirits, some of them very mischievous indeed. Things tended to happen around my slot that didn't seem in keeping with the rest of the programme. One night just as I was finishing, one of the huge lights exploded giving us all, including the viewers, quite a fright! The spirits of the nursing staff seemed contented to be there but some of the spirit patients seemed very disturbed! There was one happy chap though who used to zoom about in his spirit wheelchair between make up, green room and studio as though he was one of the station's staff. Others could feel the breeze as his wheelchair whooshed past and he seemed happy that I could see him. Tuesday nights became filming nights for the next two years of my life.

I had been working for Lanarkshire TV for a few months when I received a call from a producer at Pearson Television in London to see if I wanted to audition for a show called Mystic Challenge which they were making for UK Living channel. At first I thought it was a joke. The 'audition' was to give one of the producers a phone reading simply using my tarot to pick up things about her. I had never done phone readings and wasn't sure how it would work but I said yes and we arranged for a time that suited us both the next day. I remember sitting

62

on the floor in my house with the cards in front of me wishing that I had said no as I was obviously going to be rubbish. I was worried that I might not hear properly too. The phone rang and a lovely lady asked me if I could simply tell her a bit about her life. Mystic Challenge was a show where celebrities who were completely hidden were read for by two psychics who battled against one another and were judged by a studio audience led by a journalist who had been in the room when the readings had been done. So I needed to be able to read without actually interacting with someone. This information made a phone reading sound like a piece of cake!!

I simply went for it. I picked up quite a few things including the woman's skin tone and about her childhood. Then some things which I thought were general but maybe weren't because by the end of the phone call she said that it was brilliant and she was inviting me onto the show! She explained that Paul Ross was the presenter and that if I did well in the first shows I could be invited back. Three shows would be filmed at a time in London and the fee was quite good. All expenses would be covered by Pearson TV and I was scheduled to fly down from Glasgow in three weeks' time. I had said yes before it struck me I was going to be on national TV and then I felt sick. This was way different from my astrology slot on Lanarkshire TV. I think the only thing that kept me sane was that both my daughters were so excited for me.

The Sunday evening flight from Glasgow to Heathrow Airport was full of business people heading back to London after weekends with their families. As usual I arrived early and the extra time gave my nerves free rein. 'What if I was awful and didn't get anything? What if I couldn't hear well enough? What if I got lost in London?'. The plane was packed and I waited to see who would be sitting next to me but as the doors shut I realised that the middle seat had not been taken. I thought this was good as I might have been tempted to grip my fellow passenger as we took off as I really don't like flying. The plane taxied along the runway and I felt sick with nerves. Something caught my attention from the middle seat. I looked around and there was my mum's spirit sitting in it! She was smiling and looked excited to be there. I knew then that I would be alright.

I was carried along with the crowd out towards baggage collection. (For later shows I would take hand luggage but for now I had four different outfits, three pairs of shoes and a bag full of makeup. Three tarot decks, my runes, my crystals and my crystal jewellery.) When I entered the main thoroughfare I was overcome with anxiety because it was so busy and I couldn't hear the public address system properly which seemed to be giving out instructions continually. I had been told I would be met: but where? How? Then I saw something that made me laugh. There was a row of chauffeurs all dressed in black holding big signs with peoples' names on. My married name then was Halket. The Universe was playing a joke though because my sign simply said 'Hellcat'. I knew it was my chauffeur because I was used to all sorts of misspelling. But I never had Hellcat before!

I was dropped off at a fancy hotel and almost jumped up and down on the extra soft bed with more cushions than I had seen in my life. My en-suite was stunning and I immediately did the 'tourist thing' and resolved to take all the toiletries home with me for my girls. From there it was a wonderful dinner eaten by myself in a lavish dining room, all paid for by Pearson TV. The lounge was full of business types socialising but I went up to my room to prepare for an early start the next morning. I was on an adventure and enjoying it very much. I was picked up by another chauffeur after breakfast and was taken into Pearson TV via a side door. This was the first indication that this was a serious show. I was given my own 'runner', a person who would bring me anything I needed and was told that I couldn't move without her. All the psychics who were here to record were kept way from any areas that the celebrities were in. In fact, we weren't allowed to go to the loo or for a smoke unless our runner checked on mobile phones first that the coast was clear. The enormity of it all hit me when I was ushered into the room the other psychics were in. Most were names I knew already from the TV or magazines and all looked quite calm. Some had been part of the first series and had been invited back. I caught sight of my favourite astrologer David Wells and nerves hit me. Oh god, surely I wouldn't be up against David? I would surely lose.

I was introduced to everyone and took my seat as we waited for the first two psychics to be called for the first celebrity. There were about eight of us. One man who I won't name because he was so unimportant that I actually can't remember his name, looked me up and down. He said, 'You'll do fine. The main issue you'll have is that TV adds a stone on you so you are going to look very big.' I couldn't believe he had made a joke about my weight! He wasn't exactly slim line himself. I could feel White Storm at my back and I looked back at the man with my guide's strength behind me. I realised that he was psyching me out! He was trying to make me lose before I had even competed! And this man was meant to be spiritual? He also decided we should all tell the group our sun signs. Most people were water signs e.g. Pisces, Scorpio or Cancer. When I piped up that I was the earth sign Taurus, Mr 'Spiritual' joked that I didn't stand a chance among all the intuitive water signs. At that point my Taurean bull came into play and vowed to prove him wrong! By the end of nine shows of Mystic Challenge, I had won seven!

He was the only arse. The rest were lovely. David Wells introduced himself and said he had heard good things about me. I was chuffed to bits. We weren't to be pitched against one another and were being called in an hour so we sat down with more coffee. That was the beginning of a friendship that has lasted till this day. David was as nervous as I was and a sweeter guy you will never find. We resolved to meet up later. Next it was make up and I was amazed as the makeup artist wiped out my features and then put them back on stronger, more intense and very beautifully. I feel this is where my love of makeup really started. Then it was a short meditation and up to the room where I would 'read' for my first celebrity. I sat down with a journalist at the back of me who was there to make sure that there was no sharing of info or cheating. Then the assistant brought in a celebrity covered from head to foot in a big black cloak. I thought I would burst out laughing as he/she tripped over the chair as he could see nothing. Even the shoes were covered. And then it started:

My first celebrity shuffled my cards as best as possible though the material and before long my Rohrig deck was giving me images and my guide was urging me on. I heard some sort of starting pistol and felt some sort of race. Then I saw a man in silk pyjamas and made a joke that he liked his bed. I picked up things about charity and age etc. but I couldn't really pull then together. Then he was ushered out and the assistant handed me her notes and asked me to sign them in front of the journalist. They were then typed up and given back to me. Then me and my competitor who had also read for the same celebrity were placed in a room behind sliding doors and had headphones on while the guest was introduced by Paul Ross in the studio. The music played was meant to be calming but I felt I was going to wet myself. Then a dry ice machine was switched on and the head phones came off and Paul Ross introduced me as simply 'Colette from Scotland'. By this time the celebrity was behind another wall in front of the studio audience waiting to react on camera to what we had sensed about him. This structure was used on all the shows and after a while I got used to it.

I stumbled making my way sit beside Paul Ross. Typical I thought. Then the camera was on me and I read word for word what was on my signed notes. We had one minute to say as much as we could. Then I moved over a seat and my competitor did the same. Then the studio audience who knew who the celebrity was announced the winner. I lost my first show. The celebrity was Bob Champion and my competitor won because he intuited there was a film about him. I accepted defeat with good grace still delighted that I had got through the first show. Later on I realised that if I had just let my intellect work with my intuition I could have realised that it was a jockey! Silk pyjamas, starting pistol and race!

I won my second show and again had another lesson that my guide was providing me with direct answers. My mystery celebrity was Billy Murray who is an actor who starred in a TV police show, The Bill. I got that he was an actor and had links to the police as I saw flashing lights on a police car. I sensed some dodgy connections- he was friendly with the Kray twins in real life! I got lots of other things but what I didn't put together was something so frustrating for my guide that I thought he would walk away and never come back. He told me to draw out two cards for explanation in the reading. One card that came out was The Sun card. The other was the Ace of Discs which has a big hill on it. But much as I said it over and over, I didn't realise the words Sun and Hill were important and well known! The police station in which the TV show was set was called Sunhill. I sometimes wonder if White Storm rues the day he gifted himself to me as a guide!

The other show I lost was a singer called Carol Decker from the 80s group T'Pau. I had such a lot on her but the other psychic felt drawn to the country or word 'China'. T'Pau's massive hit had been 'China in Your Hand'. Fair do's! My favourite celebrity was a massive win for me. I sensed a male who was so creative, loved fashion, who also had an amazing singing voice, was associated with royalty and for whom English wasn't his first language. I also felt he had a scar above his left eyebrow. Seeing David Emmanuel freak out at this later on video as I said it was so funny. He designed Princess Diana's wedding dress, his first language is Welsh, he was part of a choir that had a record out. And yes, he did have a scar above his left eyebrow! I genuinely felt that I had shown my gift well.

I went up and down to London a few times to record more Mystic Challenge shows. I kept winning but after nine shows I had done enough. I was still seeing clients, writing my columns, doing my Lanarkshire TV slot and running workshops. I was exhausted. I read for Trevor Sorbie who is adorable, Fey Presto who is a transvestite magician and had both male and female energies. There was also a female world champion sky diver. And someone who although obviously very famous also gave me the creeps. I had picked up that one celebrity was a 'mother hen' type of person who was responsible for other people's reputations. He was well known for this skill but I couldn't place him and was happy when the reading finished. The man was Max Clifford, the PR guru, who was convicted of child abuse many years later.

When Mystic Challenge aired I was stopped in the street a lot in Hamilton and congratulated. It was a lot of fun and I enjoyed the experience. I also had made a lifelong friend in David. We also met up as by that time we had the same agent. Some opportunities were opening up to me but my marriage was ending and I was simply a mess. One of the opportunities involved relocating to London for a new TV show with a great fee. I was excited but in my heart felt that I couldn't uproot my children from their dad and family and friends. My spiritual elder was in Scotland at the time so I asked him what he felt on it. He simply said 'Colette, not every opportunity needs to be yours.' I have repeated this to many clients over the years who have been conditioned by our culture that every opportunity should be followed or we are in some way letting ourselves down. It is one of the best pieces of advice I have ever been given.

A few years later I had had forgotten about Mystic Challenge but it was sold to a new channel called Challenge TV and was aired in a loop for nearly two years! I wish I had a percentage rather than a straight fee!

.

10

I had dreamed of having my own premises for my clairvoyant career. The house parties were enjoyable but you never knew what you were going to find. One night could be an amazing night in in a poor area with wonderful people who looked after you like you were a queen. Those nights made you feel as though you had really helped. Others might be in a big home with much comfort where you were aware that you were some sort of sideshow. I always held the same ethics in my clairvoyant practice as I had in my pharmacy practice. I gave everyone the same amount of time and courtesy whether they were wealthy or not. So I hated being called the 'fortune teller' and treated like some sort of oddity. I was a clairvoyant consultant and if I wasn't treated well I simply would never go back. Also some houses were simply more comfortable to read in than others. In one home I had the whole of the extension to myself with heating and lots of treats. In another home I would be given a tiny space at a breakfast bar and had to perch on a stool for five hours. In one home it was so poor that I had a one bar fire on in deep winter in the baby's damp room and wondered how the wee thing could thrive. She didn't. I saw some grand homes and such poverty. All clients were treated with the same respect and concern.

The house parties were a great learning experience. I usually knew whether I would love a place or hate it within seconds of being greeted. There were also some amazing experiences that have stayed with me forever. In one house I was reading in a child's room which was perfect with no toys out of place and I felt so many spirits around me. The mum came in last for her reading and I was suddenly aware that this room had been a haven to a child who had passed into spirit. It seemed to flood with light when the mum came in. I sense a wee girl and told her that I felt her daughter was here. Her eyes filled up and I felt her sadness. I was just about to lean forward to hug her when a little toy duck which was on a high shelf started to go 'quack, quack, quack!' The mum looked up in shock and the duck started quaking again. It was her daughter's favourite toy. I laughed and said, 'Oh well something has set the duck off,' and she said that it had a switch that you had to put to 'on' before the duck would quack. I was always very practical so I said that maybe a vibration had flicked the switch. She said yes that's true. I said though that maybe it could be her daughter and the duck quacked again! I was quite delighted for her. I was left shocked though when she told me that she had taken the batteries out of the duck a few months earlier so even if the switch had flicked, there were no batteries in it to make it quack! The wee girl was certainly a strong spirit.

I had a terrible experience in another house where I was again placed in a child's room. I felt very queasy and uncomfortable and felt that I would ask to move to another room. Before I could ask I 'saw' the image of a child being abused by a man on the bed in the room. It sickened me. I called the mum in and asked if I could be moved. She looked at me and said, 'Do you feel it or did you see it?' I said I saw it. She started to cry and said, 'He was a family member. We trusted him. He has been charged and is going to trial soon. Will my daughter ever be okay?' I hugged her and moved to another room. Before I left I cleansed and blessed the room the abuse had taken place in. The family couldn't move house. This was their home but I was determined that the wee one's room would not be tarnished by such a strong bad imprinted psychic memory. I often wondered why I was put in that room. It could have been simply the most accessible but I wonder too if it was some sort of test.

Most tarot parties went on far too long. I was never good at keeping to time. So I might go home at about 1am and be wired to the moon. It would take a glass of wine and some reading before I could go to bed. Then maybe I would be up the next day for my pharmacy job. I was wearing two hats: a science one and a paranormal one. It wasn't easy. One day I was in my pharmacy and I realised that I had my tarot deck in the pocket of my white coat which was ludicrous. Spirit was calling me and I knew I should follow. My guide said to me that one day I would know why walking away from pharmacy and serving spirit would be good for me too. I now know what he meant. My hearing deteriorated over the years and I now have two hearing devices, can't hear on the phone or in busy environments. I would have had to give up pharmacy at one point as I would have been a danger to my patients especially if I had to phone a doctor to confirm a medicine dose. So in following spirit, I was gifted a career that eventually would be able to be adapted for my hearing loss.

After my mum died I knew that I would eventually have the courage to move towards my dream. Yet it was scary. I had a good job in a lovely pharmacy in the south side of Glasgow doing a job share with an old friend. The money was good and the chap I worked for was a colleague from my old Scott Chemist days. But I had changed. I wanted to try to see if I could succeed. I had thought about renting somewhere in Cambuslang where I lived but felt it was better not to live and work in the same area. Rutherglen looked good but I saw that as Leandra's territory and he had been a help to me so I felt it would have been wrong to open up in some sort of competition. I decided just to wait until the right place came along. I knew I would know.

In September of 1996 I was walking down Quarry Street in Hamilton when I looked up and saw a poster in a second floor window saying there were offices to rent. I just 'knew'. I immediately climbed the stairs to find that the whole of the top floor on the right was leased to an engineering firm who wanted to sublet two offices to the back of the building and share a toilet and waiting area/hall. . The place smelt of men and oil and machinery, dirty work-boots and filing cabinets but it didn't put me off. Even the toilet didn't put me off. This was where I was meant to be! Little did I know that I was in the right building but actually on the wrong floor which would be rectified within months. I signed a six month lease and began preparing my wee offices and making leaflets and accruing chairs and tables and nice curtains and feminine things that I am sure drove the engineers mad. I don't think they had ever had a scented candle burning in the waiting area. The toilet was transformed too with flowers and clean towels and even toilet rolls!

All this preparing was done during the day on my days off from my pharmacy career. By October 1996 I was ready to launch 'Colette Clairvoyant' complete with my 'eye' logo which has been synonymous with me ever since. The first few clients were during the day. I had taken a little advert out in the local paper, bought a new-fangled mobile phone and felt lucky that the weeks were filling up with clients. I had a good base to start with but it seemed lots of people didn't like to have clairvoyants to their homes and welcomed one in town centre offices. My diary was very healthy. I was working day time and a few nights. This allowed me to get Jennifer out to school and pick her up at 3pm. And leave the girls with their dad two nights a week. I found Jill a wonderful nursery in Motherwell for a few days a week.

It was looking great until I went in to do my first evening session. I was two flights up in an old tenement building. The tiled stair wells were lovely with large stained glass windows on each landing. But on my first night there were no lights on. I initially thought it was a power cut and I would have to cancel the clients as two flights of unlit stairs were an accident waiting to happen. It was a commercial property and I was the only one in the building at night. The group of three women were already on their way when I phoned the home of one. So I decided to be resourceful and lined each stair with a lit tea light and put large pillar candles on the window ledges. It looked amazing: very spooky and mysterious but unfortunately didn't really light the stairs that much. So I found a torch and led my three clients upstairs all hanging on to one another for dear life. I was so stressed I wondered if I would be able to read for them. But once in I closed the door, made us all coffee, did a short meditation and had a very accurate and enjoyable night. The joy of the readings lasted only as long as it took to realise that by the time they were due to leave that all the tea lights on the stairs had gone out and it was pitch black and we were still two floors up. I had used all my tea-lights. I was thankful in my head that I had Public Liability insurance as I led the three women back down two flights of stairs with one torch and a few pillars candles in each landing. It was an experience I would never, ever want to have again. The ladies were wonderful and were happy to have had their readings but I was a wreck. I was even more of a wreck when I realised that once again I had to go back upstairs to lock up. I was very aware of being on my own totally in the dark. I wasn't afraid of ghosts or spirits. I was scared of someone being in the close with me. In my hurry to get back to the safety of my office, I tripped and cut my leg. I burst into tears in my office. It had been a wonderful but also dreadful night.

The following morning I phoned the engineers to tell them about the power cut and explain why there were used tea lights and candles all over the stairs. My heart fell when they told me that it hadn't been a power cut. The building was commercial property and the stairwell lights went off at six o'clock every evening! I remember being quite precise in what I said next - either get the lights on for me the next day or I would rescind my lease and go elsewhere. They had to approach the landlord who then had to send his handyman to the building to set new timers for the lights. I simply couldn't believe that a whole building had no lighting at night. There was a firm of tech specialists on the first floor and a goldsmith. Did they never work at night?

The lights were fixed and I proceeded to enjoy my new offices. The men were loud and had rather choice language and the secretary hoovered when I had clients in which struck me as odd. Yet once I explained my problem to her she changed her hoovering schedule and sometimes could be heard shushing the men up with, 'Colette has a client'. The place felt good. I was learning not to take myself so seriously as the engineers had a good line in 'funny' comments like, 'You didn't see that coming' or, 'So…tell me the lottery numbers?' Initially it was annoying but after a while I simply took it with the fun which it was meant.

I started writing a column for the Motherwell and Hamilton People in January 1997. This column lasted nineteen years. My diary was fine and I didn't need to do pharmacy locum work. The outgoings were a lot even though it was a sublet but I was happy enough. I decided it would be good to run some psychic development classes which filled up right away. I wrote a short six week course and off we went. The smaller office was a good enough space to have about ten people and every week we tried a tool of divination or learned a new psychic skill. Each session had a tutorial followed by a demonstration and then they would have to try it themselves .It was all women and they were such a talented bunch that I felt totally blessed to have their company. This was the start of the building of my psychic soul family: those people who needed a Colette in their life. I, in turn, needed them for my development as a teacher and mentor.

One night I taught tea leaf readings. One night we did the runes. One was a basic intro to the tarot. We did pendulums and divining rods. It was a very old building and one of my great joys was the divining to sense 'cold' spots where spirit energies were. I taught the ladies how to make divining rods with a wire coat hanger and two straws. Then they walked slowly around the offices and screamed and jumped when the rods went crazy crossing over one another when they hit a spirit spot. Then the rods would uncross as they moved away from it. All of this was not coming from them as the rod handles were placed in drinking straws so that they could spin and move without any interference. I remember that night as one of my favourites ever. It spurred me on to write a course on the tarot which became a diploma in Tarot Studies which was launched by my new tarot school, the Scottish School of Tarot. But first I would move premises again.

.

11

First floor, front office - 90 Quarry Street, Hamilton. My new offices marked a time of real spiritual and professional progress. They were just down stairs from my original offices. The tech engineers were doing very well and decided to move to more modern offices. Their offices were to the front with a great view of Quarry Street when it was a bustling wee hive of activity. One day Natalie, the goldsmith who shared the floor with them came up and said that they were moving out and she was looking for someone she liked to take over rather than someone new and who maybe wouldn't fit in with the ambiance of her work and showroom. I understood this because her work was simply amazing. She was so talented. This planted a seed in my head so I booked a meeting with my landlord who owned the whole side of the building. It was a bigger space all round and cost quite a bit more but I reckoned it would be a good place to be. The offices themselves were clean and bright and didn't need anything done to them. So after six months of being on the top floor to the back, I moved to the first floor at the front. I put my posters with my now symbolic psychic eye logo on the windows and immediately became more noticed. I had started writing for The Lanarkshire People newspapers and my column was bringing more people towards me and bookings were good. Money was tight though as overheads were high and I had moved twice in seven months.

The new office space shared the hall/waiting area with Natalie and her clients were discerning and knew what they wanted. She attracted some high earners and it wasn't long before some of them booked in with me too. So as well as my normal, everyday clients, I started to attract businessmen and women, footballers and the odd celebrity. I feel that they had a degree of anonymity as they could simply have been waiting in the waiting area for a meeting with Natalie, the goldsmith. It wasn't long though before I realised that I was doing well with business readings. I feel this was due to my clairvoyance but also because I had run pharmacies and understood the world of business. Also, due to a lack of knowledge of football, I would sometimes be totally clueless that I was reading for someone well known until I actually had their cards out in front of me. This was a time where I would also see the odd politician, celebrity or socialite. I feel that they enjoyed their readings with me because I have never really been that impressed by money or celebrity. Everyone got the same warm welcome and sometimes, a good telling off! I was working flat out. I had given up a good salary as a pharmacist of about £27,000. Due to the overheads and changing over of leases etc. my net profit for my first year as a clairvoyant was £9,000. Yet I never considered going back the way and am glad I stayed the course as it has given me such a happy contented life. It isn't all about money! Although we were eating Farmfoods meals and my car was a bit of a disaster. This was the year where I learned how to be very frugal.

The only downside initially was that the goldsmith's diamond grinder made the most ridiculous noise and sometimes proved a distraction in readings. One day I had a headache with it and was so annoyed I literally wished it would just stop. And it did. Natalie had to call an engineer out see what was wrong. He was baffled as he said that all the parts were able to move, the power supply was fine but he simply couldn't get it to work either. He joked that maybe it was having a 'witchy woman' across the hall from it. He went away to see if he could get more help on it. The next day I felt so sorry that Natalie had so much work to do and her main machine wasn't working. I said a wee prayer that all would be OK and promised that I would find a way of dealing with the noise. When Natalie opened up that morning and switched her machine on, it worked.

I settled into my lovely offices well. Jill was at a nursery three days a week and I became a bit of a celebrity around Hamilton. One day in the glorious summer, I left Jennifer and Jill playing in the garden with their dad looking after them, and set off for work along the M74. My first husband's niece Helen, who had died tragically at the dentist, use to join me in the car sometimes. She would also help out in readings especially when it was for a parent who had lost a child. She was maturing as a spirit and was more relaxed with me than when she was alive. I was looking forward to working knowing that it was a lovely summer night and my girls would be playing outside with their friends and would be put to bed by their dad while I worked.

I was half way along the M74 when Helen, who had manifested in the passenger seat beside me, suddenly yelled 'Jillian' and promptly disappeared. I nearly crashed the car in fear. I knew that Helen would not have left like that if something hadn't been truly wrong. I took the first turn off and used my mobile phone to call home. No answer. I rang again. Still no answer. I started to do a U-turn to get back on the motorway. I phoned again. No answer. Just before I headed back home I rang home again and this time my husband answered.

I sobbed down the phone, 'Is she okay?' and he said, 'Yes, but I don't know how.' Basically Jill had been on her little trike bike and had gone out of the garden onto the wee lane at the back of the houses. There were neighbours in the gardens across and they saw her pick up speed and head towards the road. We lived in a very quiet cul-de-sac with very little traffic. My neighbour said that she stood up and started to run towards Jill on her bike but Jill reached the end of the pavement and her and her bike went into the path of a taxi. My neighbour said that what happened next freaked her out. Jill's bike hit the side of the taxi and instead of going under its wheel it kind of bounced off the taxi, rotated and threw her back onto the pavement. She said it was like some sort of miracle. She said that someone must have been looking after Jill. I knew exactly who had been looking after her: Helen, her big cousin in Spirit. I will be forever in her debt. Jill was shocked and a bit grazed but nothing that her dad couldn't sort out.

This incident led me to believe that we should never, ever call a spirit. As a medium I would ask for anyone who wanted to pass on messages to do so. This is different to asking for a spirit's name and willing them forward. That is necromancy. What if Helen had been summoned by some person on earth just at the time she had saved my daughter from an accident or worse? What if she had been distracted by someone calling her name to come visit at that time? This is why we should never call on, or will, a spirit forth. They could be needed elsewhere.

Many of my clients had expressed interest in my very practical way of reading that tarot. I decided to write a tarot course and in October 1997 The Scottish School of Tarot was born. The course was accredited by the professional body provisionally. It just had to have one of my students take the governing body's exam for full accreditation. I was very proud of the course and the twelve places filled virtually overnight. It was a ten month/ ten module diploma course run every second Monday with homework for the weeks in between. It was quite a difficult course which focused on not just learning the cards but on ethics and professionalism. The first group were amazing and I so enjoyed teaching them the tarot archetypes in a way that they would understand them. I compared them to people and places and events that they would know and you could see the penny drop and final understanding. It gave me so much pleasure. As the weeks built my little group became friends and allies. I became a passionate teacher and mentor sometimes taking so much time correcting homework that financially I was working for far less than minimum wage!

The course was written about in a few newspapers including the Glasgow Evening Times, The Scotsman picked up on it as did The Daily Record. I was delighted. So I was mystified when I was asked by Leandra, the clairvoyant who initially foresaw my clairvoyance, to visit him to talk about my Tarot School. When I arrived he said he was going to be very honest with me and was going to ask me to shut my tarot school down. He said it would be for my own good. I was totally confused as I felt he would have supported me. He was old and I felt that he should be glad that more people would be trained in the art of the tarot as he was a wonderful reader and clairvoyant/astrologer. He said he was acting on behalf of a couple of psychics who felt my tarot school would affect their income. I was stunned. The two psychics were far more well-known than me and I felt that they would not be affected at all because many of my students were simply learning for themselves and those who did go on to be professional would simply not be charging the fees for a reading that these two did. I had learned the tarot by myself and wished so often that there had been a class or

78

mentor for me. Why didn't they feel that passing on knowledge was a good thing?

Leandra then passed on a threat. He said to remember that, 'Tall poppies are cut down if they grow too tall.' He told me a story of a man who had gotten on the wrong side of the male psychic who opposed him and it was very scary. Me being me though, I told him I wasn't afraid of the man and to pass on that I would not shut my Tarot school down. I left his apartment that night so disappointed and I never saw him again. Leandra passed a few years ago. I still have fond memories of his initial encouragement of me.

A few days later I was summoned by the female clairvoyant who was against my school for a 'wee chat'. Basically the wee chat was once again a demand to close my tarot school. I couldn't understand her concerns about it affecting her. She was a good clairvoyant with a great business. So once again I stood up for my work and said that I would not shut my Tarot school. I drove home slightly winded by the whole experience. Within 24 hours I was in bed feeling like a heavy weight was on my chest and I couldn't breathe. I had to cancel that week's tarot school. I felt like I had the worst flu ever and had no idea how I would even look after my daughters. One of the friends I was in touch with on the internet via a forum emailed me and asked me if I was all right. She sensed something bad had happened to me and felt I needed her magick. I explained how I felt and she asked me to consider that I had been put under psychic attack. I knew she was right. I had been warned to shut my tarot school and had said No! Now I was being made ill and the outcome would probably be the same.

I hadn't realised how many magickal friends I had. Within days they had formed a group and were doing ritual to break the bad intent. I was sent a parchment with Solomon's Seal to wear on me; those who were devoted to angels sent their prayers to angels. It was like a force of good circled round me and protected me with their energy. I will always be grateful to them. I felt better within a few days. I could move my body without feeling trapped by a giant rock. The whole incident left me not only even more determined that my tarot school would be a success, but determined to learn more about protection magick so that I would never , ever be vulnerable again. In fact one of the great blessings in all of this is that I moved forward into the world of magick and eventually started to teach that too. My tarot school lasted until I chose to work from home and then became an online course. Then it became a bestselling book. But I will never, ever forget the lesson in vulnerability and also that even in a spiritual community, people can work in ways which aren't that spiritual. I wouldn't say that they were bad people: maybe just misguided and over reacting to a perceived threat to their livelihoods. I still have a good place in my heart for Leandra who I believe was only the messenger because he knew me. In some ways I was a naive wee girl but that changed after I had felt just how awful a psychic attack could be. In all my magickal life I have never, ever put anyone under psychic attack even though I know how to do it. I do however believe in reflecting bad intent back to source so it hits the one that sent it.

Business continued to boom in my premises with readings and workshops and lots of media projects. I started writing for the Sunday Sun in England as their astrologer following Russell Grant's departure. I had an astrology phone line. It was good. My marriage wasn't thriving though and I separated from my husband in 1998 for six months. It was a time of great emotional upheaval. At the same time the landlord of the other half of the building changed it from commercial to residential. At first it was OK and I was happy to not be the only person in the whole building at night. But it began to go downhill. The people across the way had a dog and they let it mess the close every morning. It was a huge dog and its mess was huge. I had to clean it up before clients arrived. Then at night their presence became rowdier and I could hear it when I was reading for clients. Some nights there would be brawls outside my door. Natalie's workshop was broken in to. One night I had a group of four women in for readings. I was barely through the first reading when some idiot started kicking in our outer door. He was swearing and out of control. I think he was looking for the people next door who were out. I gathered the women into my back room and called the police but he got in and started to be threatening. He only stopped when he saw Natalie's security cameras. I knew that I couldn't risk clients' wellbeing and sadly started to look for new premises. I will always have fond memories of both my Quarry Street premises but the first floor ones marked a massive leap in my business and also proved to be an amazing time for spiritual growth.

INTERLUDE

MY PSYCHIC TOOLBOX

I have always had a natural psychic gift but learned very early on that using a 'tool' as such could bring extra accuracy and understanding. I have studied and learned about many forms of divination in my life and tried many out. Some were more successful than others but each has had its own fascination and intensity. I have enjoyed learning about each one and have also enjoyed teaching the ones I felt strongly connected to and that became part of my day to day practice. In fact my interest in divination led to my book How To Read An Egg, which was a look at divination tools, both weird and wonderful. There are so many ways to divine information out there but all need the practitioner to have psychic ability and knowledge to use them. When I see someone with a natural clairvoyant ability who is developing and feeling overwhelmed by it, the first thing I suggest they do is to 'find' their tool of the trade and them make themselves a toolbox. I know this sounds very practical but you wouldn't expect a plumber to fix your blocked drain without some tools. He may know instinctively how to do it and maybe could do it with his bare hands but it would be easier, quicker and done with more precision if he had his toolbox with him and could select a plunger! I believe that psychic readings are the same.

My first tool of divination was never bought with that intention. It was a lovely Celtic Crystal paperweight with swirls and designs imprinted on to the glass in black. It was beautiful and I believe I bought it on the isle of Mull. When I first practiced face to face psychic reading I realised that I needed something to connect me to the client.

When I was a student I had done 'palm' readings that were really just divining information by holding the persons hand, but hands can be sweaty, sticky and warm and I was always aware that some people just didn't feel comfortable having their hands held. So I thought a 'Colette' form of psychometry would be good. Instead taking the persons hand or asking for some jewellery from then, I would get them to hold something for a few minutes and then I would connect with them by holding it in my palm. The nearest thing to hand was my Celtic paperweight! This seemed to delight people and while they sat with eyes closed holding it I could see them relax and could have a wee peek at their aura.

But something magickal happened! Instead of just feeling things from the crystal and seeing visions, the crystal itself started to give answers. If someone asked about a relationship my eyes would be drawn to either a connected swirl or a dead end swirl. My intuition had already given me an answer and it always matched up with what the crystal showed. So I decided to really look at what was in the crystal and see what each swirl told me. Then I memorized it and when it showed it to me in a reading, then I had my answer. So the paperweight became a personal tool of divination which I had developed just for me. It sounds weird but it worked well and people loved the crystal itself. I still have it. It taught me a lot about scrying, psychometry but mainly that absolutely anything could be used for divination as long as you let the Universe know that intend to use it. It was the other way round with me-the Universe let me know that the crystal could be used.

I had purchased my first tarot deck, Tarot Balbi, and had learned the tarot from it and many books . I wanted to incorporate it into my readings but felt that I wanted to become totally confident and knowledgeable in the tarot before I used it for a client. So I continued my tarot studies over years while using my Celtic crystal. I felt I needed some sort of less complicated oracle deck though so I bought PsyCards which proved to be a good half way house. Psycards have forty cards instead of the seventy-eight of the tarot and have a 'Yes', 'No', and 'Maybe' card. This allowed for more specific answers than the Celtic crystal and paved the way for me using my tarot deck when I was happy I knew enough. I would say that I took about four years to learn and practice the tarot before I used it on anyone other than friends and family. I was self-taught through books and meditations- there was no internet back then!

So my readings developed around the Celtic crystal and Psycards. Then I replaced Psycards with the Tarot. I leaned with Tarot Balbi but soon bought a very pretty deck called Hanson Roberts. It is quite cute and has appealing images that clients seemed to like. I had also developed an interest in Runes and used a few runes at the end of readings to give timings or lucky advice. I became very interested in Norse spirituality and all the old Norse myths and legends. I spent many nights reading about Odin, Balder, Freya and Frigga and of course Loki. All the while I was practicing pharmacy while learning and optimizing my psychic skills. I only launched my first business and gave up pharmacy when I felt that I had both the skills and the toolbox to allow me to be the best reader I could be. Of course any clairvoyant will tell you that they are quite open to acquiring new baubles and I had a good selection of tarot decks by then with runes and oracle decks thrown in too.

I was asked one night by a woman at a house party about a form of divination that they assumed I was using and hadn't seen before. The woman was last in and said that the women downstairs were excited to know what the white pebbled like objects were that were at the edge of my reading space. They were fascinated because after each reading, one seemed to disappear! I started off with a little pile but by the end of the night they had been used up. They had never seen 'stones' like them before as they had no markings and were intrigued. This caught me off guard because I wasn't aware of anything other than tarot and runes on my table. But the woman was adamant- I had at least six white stones to my left at the beginning of the night. She wanted to know my secret. Then it came to me with a flash what she meant and I couldn't help but laugh. I put a little pile of Softmints out at the beginning of the session and after each client I ate one or two to refresh my mouth!! My secret divination method was SOFTMINTS! That caused a lot of laughter and I still chuckle at it today when I buy my Softmints.

I also tried to read the ribbons. I was interested in colours and also felt that by asking the client to hold one end of a ribbon she had chosen while I held the other end that I was tuning in well. I acquired a crystal ball and tried scrying. It was a time of experimentation and joyful learning but bit by bit I honed my tarot skills and was ready to move forward with a reading type that I still use to this day. I had discovered the Rohrig Tarot and felt I had come home. This deck spoke to my heart and rearranged my thoughts on certain cards and meanings. My guide also connected to it very well and my clients loved it even though it was quite naughty in places. Rohrig was giving me answers like no other deck and my guide seemed to be able to manipulate them. We developed a way of reading that used the tarot as a conversation between him, me and the client. Basically I did a yearly reading and then used Rohrig to answer questions. I didn't follow a set spread but instead allowed White Storm to tell me how many cards to put out and what pattern to put them out in. This was done for every question and was intense and exhausting but so very, very accurate. It meant that my readings became longer and more in depth and I stopped 30 minute readings and moved to 60 minute ones. I just couldn't keep to time. Luckily I had premises by then and had stopped house parties which would never have worked with longer readings. The original Rohrig is not in print anymore and because of this the deck is valuable in money terms but to me it is priceless. There are Argentinian fakes available which are awful. The colours are all wrong. I believe you can still purchase a Spanish deck which is authentic. I do hope that Carl Rohrig will allow his cards to be reprinted at some point. They are so beautiful and have so many stunning visuals in each card.

I bought a crystal ball to see if I could scry but found it too tiring on my eyes. So it sat on my reading table for a few years more as a decoration than anything else. It had cost quite a bit of money but made for good photos for articles I wrote or was featured in in newspapers and magazines. Yet it was superfluous as a psychic tool but it played its part in allowing me to attend a spiritual event which I really wished to go to but hadn't enough money. I had wanted to go to a sweat lodge site in England to see some old friends and experience a new teacher. The weekend was to cost me £65 but I was struggling financially due to marriage pressures and the centre I ran not doing so well. So I decided to just give the intent up to Spirit and if I was meant to attend the spiritual weekend then I knew the money would come. Two days before the event a man came for a reading. He was fascinated by my crystal ball and said it was a lovely one. I said I didn't really use it anymore and he asked if he could buy it. I knew it had a price tag of about £120 but he offered £65! The exact price of my weekend away. He went away with my crystal ball and I had a very meaningful and life changing weekend in England.

So now I have a very basic toolkit for readings. It consists of a Norse tarot Deck, A Shapeshifter tarot deck, my runes, my large Rohrig deck, my fluorite crystal necklace, some white sage, a notebook and pen and my MP3 recorder. White sage is burned to cleanse and protect my reading area and also to give short aura cleansings if the client needs it. I may also choose a crystal to give the client if I know it will help them. I have a large collection of working crystals and also ones to give away but most of them are tumble stones and not expensive points or large pieces. I don't use my crystals for divination. I use them to aid my concentration and to help the client become open or help in their healing. I have favourites and have now pared down my crystals to what I need. Most spiritual people would be wise to look at their collections of crystals/oracle decks/tarot decks/etc. and once in a while try to be more minimalist! It can be done. Pass them on to someone who would benefit from them. Don't hoard for a rainy day. I have had such joy over the years in giving things away that I bought, used and then moved on after they had shared their lesson with me. Once the lesson is learned, it is done. There is no need to have cupboards crammed with 'just in case' tools of divination or crystals.

I do have some favourite crystals which give great results in healing situations or ritual intents. I use carnelian for treating inflammation and arthritis pain; Moonstone and bloodstone for fertility issues; black obsidian for grounding and protection; snow flake obsidian for blocking bad dreams; amethyst for lessening stress and absorbing negativity; aquamarine for calming anxiety; fluorite and laboradite for opening up third eye;honey calcite for grounding in family events; citrine for confidence and happy extrovert-ism; clear quartz for alertness; sodalite for truth; Apache Tears to release tears and bottled up grief and pink quartz for keeping heart and compassion in balance. So many others to choose from but these would be in my basic kit. I am no expert by any means but always have a crystal that will do a good job in any area of life.

It has taken many years to build my psychic toolkit. Many divinatory items were used then gifted on. I now feel as though I have it perfect. I haven't bought a new tarot deck in years apart from Rohrig when I can get my hands on one. I haven't bought new crystals or runes and my pendulum is my original from ages ago. I do buy books though and I am lucky enough to be a book reviewer for a publisher so I accrue books that way too. I feel that I have my psychic toolkit but am always open to more knowledge and information. We should never stop learning!

12

1999 to 2001 was a time of endings, new beginnings and even more endings! It was possibly the most stunning time for spiritual development and personal growth but it was very stressful. I had returned to my husband after six months apart. It had been a crazy few months where I partly enjoyed my freedom but continually missed my children the weekends they were at their dad's. In fact one Saturday night in early January I left my house and knocked on his door and joined them all to watch a movie. This was bewildering to all of us. It didn't seem to make sense that we were all huddled in his small rented flat together while our family home lay empty. I simply missed family life and my husband continually told me he would change his behaviour and wanted us all back together again. I was also struggling with very strong feelings of vulnerability. I had discovered that my Scottish School of Tarot course had been sold online to someone in USA. I discovered this when they hailed me to ask for advice. I was so upset to discover that my work had been sold by someone I regarded as a friend who had actually taken the course himself and was passing himself off as a tutor. I felt sick and ended this friendship right away. This betrayal led to terrible feelings of insecurity and naivety. I was all over the place emotionally and it just seemed easier to return to my marriage. I made a decision and I was determined to make it work.

We bought a new home in Chapelhall for no other reason than it felt good and they made it very easy for us. It was a new estate and a detached house and the girls loved it. It felt like a new start but I was still uneasy that my husband's promises would disintegrate once we were back into the 9 to 5. I had to find new working premises due to the idiots next door to my Quarry Street premises. I had a lovely best friend who I had worked with in pharmacies who was also Jill's godmother. She was unhappy at work and was trying to manage an illness and one night we decided that we should open a psychic forum and she would manage it while I did my readings and workshops and promoted it. It felt really exciting and we saw very old spooky premises in Townhead Street in Hamilton that seemed to fit the bill. We had enough space to allow a few psychics to have their own rooms, and a healing room, and a very large back room which had been a store room. All of it was dilapidated and needed a lot of work which my friend was willing to tackle while I made the money for rent etc. We were caught up in the excitement and joy of having a place where like-minded people could come and learn or relax or simply be.

I made a major mistake though. I didn't listen to my own tarot cards. Before we signed the lease we decided to look at the cards for the Forum. The outcome card was one of the worst cards in the deck, The Ten of Swords. My heart sank as it came out but my friend and I decided that we could change it if we worked hard enough and committed to it enough. Two years later I had lost a lot of money but more importantly, my best friend. What started as a joy ended with arguments, recriminations and wounds that would not be mended in this life. But what a joy it was! Hamilton Psychic Forum brought joy and solace to so many people. It was place of fun and celebrations of life. It hosted events and workshops that taught us all so many new ideas. It brought new friendships that have lasted until this day. If asked, 'Would I still do it knowing what I know now?' I would probably say Yes! It was a huge learning curve for me, a time of great spiritual development and even the negatives served me well in the future. They made me stronger and wiser. Yes, the Ten of Swords, the card of misery, trauma and broken-heartedness manifested but it was balanced by so many magickal moments and wonderful memories.

My new reading room in the Forum was much smaller than my previous room but was cosy. It had a blocked out fireplace which allowed me to show off precious spiritual statues and crafts. It had room for my reading desk and chairs and also a big comfy chair for meditations before readings. It faced the back of the building so was quite quiet. It didn't take me long to settle in and enjoy my readings. Old clients followed and new ones came. My diary was very busy, booking months ahead. Yet some nights, our self-employed psychics would sit waiting for clients to turn up for readings and I felt bad for them. We had a small team of people who had applied or had been known to me for years. We had a good mix of mediums and clairvoyants but despite lots of advertising, most nights didn't fill. It was early days though and we all had a very upbeat attitude and determination to get things right.

One night I was reading for a lovely woman when her mum came through from Spirit. The woman had been crying as she missed her mum so much. It had been nearly five years but she had not stopped grieving even a little. Her mum asked me to pass on that she wanted her to stop crying all the time. This seemed to make my client worse. She cried even more. The spirit then said 'Ask her to try to stop crying and I will show her I am around her.' I passed this on and the woman dried her eyes and said that, yes if her mum wanted that, she would try. At that very moment, a glass candle holder that I had loved for years exploded into lots of shards of glass and the candle went out! My client and myself were so shocked that all we could do was stare at it and then at one another. The spirit had done what she said she would do: she had shown without doubt that when her daughter stopped crying, she had made her presence felt. We both ended up laughing and reminiscing about our bossy mums.

I remember another reading that showed me that the higher beings have a way of working which can stomp on arrogance and literally say 'told you so!' I had a businessman client who had been coming for a few years. I didn't really like him but I read for him because I felt it was important for him to see how clairvoyance worked. He always said he didn't know how I did 'my stuff' but it was always accurate. One day I was reading for him when I saw that he had a bad card out for his marriage which was in danger of ending if he didn't take more care to hide his relationship with his mistress. I am a blunt reader but it is not my place to judge anyone so I passed this on. He laughed arrogantly and said 'I have been with my mistress for years and my wife will never know.' I repeated the warning adding that it seemed that he would be found out by a very unusual and careless act. Very soon. Again he laughed. I felt a bit annoyed at him as he left as I knew he hadn't taken that part of the reading seriously although he had listened intently to the business predictions. He phoned me two days later raging that his wife had found out about his long standing affair and was leaving him and taking him to the cleaners financially. I asked how she had found out. He told me that the morning after the reading he went into his car to go to his business but his car wouldn't start. Without wakening his wife, he took her car keys and left his car at home with a view to phoning the mechanic when he got into work. He was caught up in business and hadn't time to phone. Meanwhile his wife saw her car was gone and decided to just use his to go out. When she switched on the engine it started first time and she sped away. She switched on the cassette player in the car and it started to play. Unfortunately it was the recording of her husband's reading with me from the previous day which he had listened to on his way home, only stopping at the part where I mentioned his affair. His wife heard him say that she would never find out in his arrogant, superior voice. And that was that, so they say!

I hosted an amazing night for a Native American Elder at the Forum. He was the one who introduced me to Native American spirituality and I was delighted when he was coming to Scotland again, that he agreed to come to talk to us. He was a big man. He visited my house in Chapelhall and had all the neighbourhood kids coming into our garden to see him and play with him as he held court in his Washington Redskins football cap. We found out that his great great grandmother had been Scottish and had been from a little town called 'aardry'. We then realised that he meant Airdrie and he was actually just a mile from where she lived. No such thing as coincidence! The event that night was a talk on Native American spirituality and the Earth Changes. Most of the predictions and the maps he showed us of future flooding are becoming very true as I write this. The Owl Hawk was in fine spirits, the place was sold out and it was an experience I will never forget. When the talk itself finished, he invited anyone who wished, to stay and enjoy some chants and music. About thirty people stayed even though it was after midnight, everyone was given either clap sticks or rattles or drums. Then he chanted with his own people and then had us all joining in. People who I had known to be quite shy ended up chanting and dancing and it was such a special night.

I ran a workshop on astral projection which had a few regulars at it including a man who had completed my tarot diploma and was very intuitive. I had all my students lying on the floor in a circle with their heads to the outside of it like spokes on a wheel. We were in the main hall which had been painted with planets and stars on the ceiling and had fairy lights around the walls. It was lovely. But behind one of the walls was a defunct toilet. It was never used and was disgusting with spider's webs and damp. Once my students were meditating with me, I used my voice to encourage them to see if they could lift out of their bodies even a little. My tarot student had his head to the wall which had the toilet behind him and to my horror instead of lifting up vertically from his body; he moved horizontally which meant that his aura moved through the wall and into the old toilet. I saw this and wondered if he would sense anything. Once he was back from his journey he looked puzzled and confused and asked me if I knew what was behind the wall because he felt he had been in the most awful damp disgusting toilet! Now that's talent!

So many good things happened at the Forum. So many people have thanked me for providing the space for them to grow. We held Reiki healing workshops, drum workshops, development classes, tarot classes and everyone was welcome. We kept fees down as much as possible even though we were struggling to cover our costs. It was a very busy time but my friend had some health problems and was off a lot which meant I was doing my own readings then hosting some events or taking over the reception desk at times. I was shattered. Some nights the psychics would sit all night only for a few clients to come in. It was disheartening for them. We started doing road shows where I would do the stage work and the psychics would do the readings. These were quite successful and allowed us to feel that we were providing work and they also covered some bills. But it became obvious that the main events that brought in money were out in the community and more and more the energy around the Forum itself dissipated. Some days I was in it by myself for my clients. I was paying rent and heating for a huge place when all I really needed was one room. The debt was in my name and I didn't want to accrue anymore. My good friend and I were falling apart with stress and health issues but I feel we blamed one another when really it was just circumstances. Sadly we had to be realistic and take the decision to call it a day before signing the new lease which would have locked us in for five years. We left broken, poorer and disillusioned. It truly was a Ten of Swords ending.

My life was becoming intolerable. I had to find new premises, face up to paying off a load of debt and my marriage was in its death throws. My husband's behaviour had not improved despite his promises. In fact, it had deteriorated and we spent little time together, him preferring the pub to being around me while I escaped up north to my sweat lodge site as often as I could. One night he did something that showed he had no concern for our children who he was meant to be looking after. I took my wedding ring off that night and never put it on again. The marriage was over but it took four months for us to find him a flat. Within that time we lived apart yet together. It was awful. I have so much compassion for people who have been through a drawn out separation. The Forum closed in April 2001 and my official separation started. My children, friends and my spirituality supported me. Standing Trees Medicine Lodge was still a place where we could all go for ceremony and sometimes just for time in the tepees in beautiful countryside.

Yet the time for my connection to Standing Trees was coming to an end too. We had all learned what we needed from it and the more we held on to this precious place, the more we argued among ourselves and the more we became disjointed. We had explored so many aspects of our spiritual path and were ready for new things. My health had deteriorated to the stage where I shouldn't have been doing sweat lodges at all and was asked to refrain from them until I became better. I took this so badly. My marriage had ended, my heath was bad, the Forum had failed and now I was being prevented from doing the spiritual cleansings which kept me going. Of course, the elders were right. I was simply not fit enough, due to terrible endometriosis, to partake in such a physically draining ceremony. I stayed my last solitary night in the tepee in summer 2001 and when I went home it was after saying goodbye to Standing Trees. A new cycle was beginning for me. It was as though so much had been taken from me. I was at rock bottom, yet I knew that I could make it and that there were many good things to come. I never lost my belief in Spirit: in fact it was becoming stronger than I could imagine. And White Storm was, as always, there for me.

.

INTERLUDE

SPIRITUALITY: CATHOLIC TO NATIVE AMERICAN SHAMAN

The one solid aspect of my spiritual path has been White Storm, my spirit guide. He has been with me since birth and I hope he walks with me as long as I walk on this good earth. He has been a gift from above. I don't know why I was gifted him and I wonder, if sometimes, he wonders why on earth he was gifted me! My path to the contented spiritual person I am now was fraught with deep questioning, loss of direction, dissatisfaction with religion and ultimately, surrender. I searched for answers in books, holy men, cultures but in the end it came down to following a path that simply resonated deeply within me. It also meant giving up on having to understand everything. A very wise elder once answered a young apprentice's question, 'But Grandfather, what is the Great Mystery?' with the succinct and truthful answer, 'I don't know because it *is* a Great Mystery and it wouldn't be a Great Mystery if we understood it, would it?' In the end, that made sense to me more than anything. We are spiritual beings residing in human chariots. We can't contemplate all the answers but we can get close to feeling connected to consciousness and to feel that bliss. For me, the closest answer to understanding consciousness can be found not in churches or temples but in nature. It is in nature that I am happiest. It is in water that I am most free. I feel my heart beat with the earth when I plant my spring seeds and nurture them and eat what they produce. But it was a long time before I realised that my connection to nature was my spirituality because my childhood and teens were dominated by religion.

I was born in 1961 into a Roman Catholic family. I went to a Catholic primary school and an all-girls convent secondary school. My life revolved around mass and prayers. My books were of saints who had been martyred and the catechism which I remember deep in my brain to this day.

'Who made me? God made me.

Why did God make me? God made me to know Him, love Him and serve Him in this world and the next.'

I did love Jesus so much. My dad was religious with his religion - he never missed Sunday Mass or Confession or Benediction and was part of a St Vincent De Paul society. I had a strong connection to Mary and I adored St Francis because of his love for animals. I believe he was a shaman as well as a saint! The only thing I hated about my First Holy Communion was my lace dress which itched me so much that I couldn't sit still. I later found out I was allergic to spray starch which my mum put on everything special before she ironed. I wasn't so keen on the sacrament of Confession because I felt I was telling a man my bad stuff. I never really saw priests as anything other than men who worked for Jesus and I feel that they saw that in me. It wasn't that I was disrespectful but I could see right through some of them and didn't necessarily like what I saw. I wasn't that impressed when my brother went to a seminary to study for the priesthood. In fact I remember feeling happy when he came home saying it simply wasn't for him. Then he joined the RAF which I felt was much more exciting and romantic.

I had my first shamanic experience when I was about eight which involved seeing a blade of grass vibrate and show me what it felt like to be a blade of grass. It was an awesome moment and I will never forget it. I do remember wanting to be like St Bernadette and staring at statues of Our Lady for so long, willing them to move or show me a miracle. I believed miracles existed. I felt that in my life I should be able to actually see a deity since I could already see spirits. This wasn't arrogance or my ego. I just felt different and had a belief, that although I believed in God; I had faith I would someday have proof by some sort of vision or connection. When it did come many years later it wasn't with Jesus but with the Hindu God Ganeesh and Goddess Durga. I loved Catholicism though as a child. Jesus wasn't the vengeful God that the priests told me about. He wasn't going to hurt me or send me to hell to be prodded by the devil. I never really bought into the fear and hellfire aspect of Catholicism. In my heart I knew Jesus as compassionate and peace loving.

My teens were dominated by scary nuns and forced religious practice. We had to go to Mass once a week in school and every day during Lent. I started to dislike some of the dogma of it all and held on tighter to my compassionate Jesus image. Despite this, I thought I wanted to be a nun. This came from being allowed to go sit in the convent house chapel at lunch time. I felt so contented there and I thought it was about following a religion. But looking back I see that I was meditating, escaping from the crowds of teenage girls - some of whom felt quite alien to me, and actually honing a practice of sitting still simply listening to silence. In the end I realised that I could never be a nun because I had a terrible crush on my Chemistry teacher and some very unholy thoughts! There was no internet so most of my understanding of other religions and cultures came through books. I read voraciously as a child and teenager. I read Jonathan Livingston Seagull and decided to become Buddhist. I read books about Jewish people and for a while decided I would be Jewish and study Kabbalah. I read about Russian Orthodoxy and decided I quite liked that. I watched TV shows like Kung Fu and decided I wanted to be a female Grasshopper! (Anyone under forty may have to Google this!)

My connection to other cultures was minimal. I lived in a council scheme which had Protestants and Catholics in it. In the 70s there didn't seem to be very many black or people of colour around at all so I couldn't learn from individuals. The exception to this was my wee friend Gillian who was a Mormon. Her family moved in across the road from me when I was ten. There was a general wariness of them and they kept themselves to themselves. One day Gillian came to my door and asked my mum if 'Darlene' could come out to play. My baffled mum said that no 'Darlene' lived here. Gillian was adamant. She said, 'Your daughter Darlene?' Then my mum laughed as she realised that she used to call me in for dinner by shouting, 'Darling, come in for your tea!' My mum was a wee bit posh. So I went out to play with Gillian and little by little was shown some Mormon ways. I went to her aunt's baptism and was horrified that the woman was about thirty and not a baby and was dunked in a big pool in a dress that made her look like a mermaid. I thought on it though and it made sense to be baptised when you knew what you wanted rather than when you were just a baby. After all, wasn't that what John the Baptist did?

I also liked the Mormon church which felt more like a community centre than a church. Yet I also saw a side to it that resonated with the way I saw some Catholics act. The Mormon family were known for the fact that they didn't drink alcohol or anything with caffeine in it. They didn't swear and were always well dressed and polite. Yet I saw a few family gatherings where whiskey flowed and the air was blue. They were different in church than they were at home, off duty as such. My Catholic friend had an abusive father. He would march his children to Mass on a Sunday. His wife, more often than not, couldn't come because of the two black eyes he had given her on a Friday night after he drank his pay. The family were so poor yet he guzzled whiskey and cursed for Scotland. He used Confession as a 'get out of jail free' card. I watched people and thought deeply on things even as a child. I had begun to realise that religion sometimes didn't equate with spirituality. My Gran never went to church. It was only at her death that I was told that she was Protestant before she had married my Grandad, an Irish Catholic. She brought up 13 children all as Catholics but when they were adults she simply never went to church at all. Yet she was the most compassionate and spiritual person I knew. Apart from my dad. He was spiritual while following a religion. He walked his talk, or tried to. He wasn't intolerant of other religions or cultures. He just followed his God in the way he felt and knew. He never doubted his Jesus as far as I could see. He had genuine faith until he died. But by that time I had lost my Catholic faith big style.

I feel that a great awakening for me was going to University. Strathclyde University in Glasgow was like a melting pot of skin tones and cultures in the late 70s. I was opened up to new religions I had known nothing about and also to political issues like the Palestinian/Israel problem and ethnic cleansing around the world. I sucked it all in. I read as much as I could. I talked to people. Once again, I observed. The person next to me on the pharmacy degree register was Muslim (I was F and he was G) and we were paired together for many experiments and projects. Initially I was confused by his reply to everything 'God Willing'. It drove me nuts. Even when I invited him to my wedding he said, 'Yes, God Willing.' It is only now after friendships with many other Muslims that I understand the truth in this: we can plan all we want, try all we want, but if Fate/God/Universe/whatever you want to call it has a different plan, then we are stuffed! The phrase, 'What's for you, won't go by you' has a similar vibe.

My friendships at university included a Muslim, a Sikh, a Hindu, a Wee Free Christian, and the usual Protestants and Catholics and even, say it quietly, an Atheist! We were all good friends and could chat about religion and politics with an open mind and open hearts. We didn't fall out. We didn't shoot one another or bomb one another's homes. We had respect. One of my joys was seeing a row of turbans in the church when I married my first husband. My Asian and Middle Eastern friends all turned out in their best attire and it felt truly inclusive. This was the same at my second marriage where we were honoured by a dear friend, an elderly Hindu gentleman who brought a sense of sheer holiness to the Hand Fasting ceremony. We also had a friend, Toby, in full Celtic dress who had to keep telling the children he wasn't a Viking! I spent the second part of my day out of my white wedding dress and barefoot in Native American attire with feathers in my hair. There was also a healthy mix of LGBT+ people. I have been so blessed in life to have been surrounded by so many different paths and cultures. I wish others could be more open to different religions and cultures and maybe we wouldn't have so much racism in the world and sectarianism in the West of Scotland.

I left university with far more knowledge of spirituality as well as a Pharmacy degree. I was married just after I graduated; age twenty-one, in a full Catholic ceremony. It wasn't long though until I had abandoned Sunday Mass in favour of lie-ins and without my Dad's strictness had abandoned Confession altogether. I had both my children baptised in Catholicism but left it up to them to decide later whether they wanted to pursue that religion, others or none. One is now Christian, the other is Pagan.

I feel it was my Dad's series of debilitating strokes which finally set me free from Catholic dogma. He was a good man and I was brought up to believe that if you were good and said your prayers and went to Mass and were devoted, that you would be okay. He did all these things but he very much wasn't okay. He suffered the indignity of stroke after stroke until he finally was allowed to cast off his broken body and damaged brain. Although he still had his faith right to the end, I was angry and finished with bending my knee to any God who would allow such a good man to suffer so much. The only thing I really believed in was that there was a Creator and that there was also Fate and Free Will and the rest was chaos. You could be the best person in the world and have the worst things happen to you. You could be a total arsehole and have a great life. I knew there must be more to it and that maybe, just maybe, it wasn't about just one life? The concept of Karma and past lives was starting to make sense to me. Maybe it all could balance out over many lives and it was about your soul journeys rather than just one soul journey? It was this understanding and my trusty Tarot deck that took me towards the mid Nineties and major change in both my career and understanding of my future path.

My dad died in March 1994 and my mum two years after him in 1996. I had two good years with my mum but she was tired and ready to go. Both my Mum and Dad seemed to know when they were going and had a serenity and acceptance of it. By October of 1996 I had opened my first office in Hamilton and was happily devoted to my tarot. I worked hard and in 1998 I was a bit exhausted and needed a break. I was struggling in my marriage and needed to find time to simply be me. Once I had decided to have a break, it literally fell into my lap. I was reading a spiritual magazine I was subscribed to and I dropped it and it fell open at a page telling of a Native American elder who was coming to Scotland to run some sweat lodge weekends and give talks on Native American spirituality. I felt something stir in me and booked my place right away. This one meeting was to change my life. I can honestly say after meeting this elder and taking part in teachings and ceremony that I simply knew what my path would be. The sweat lodge weekend was in a beautiful part of Scotland in a ramshackle farm but quite a few people came. There was a sense of belonging from that first night when about twelve of us slept in one tepee. It was Scotland in May. The tepee was on grass with no protection. I had brought the only sleeping bag I owned which was cheap and left me freezing cold. But it didn't matter. It just felt right. That first weekend of teachings led to me pursuing my path as often as I could and as often as finances allowed. The fact that the meeting place was up North allowed the real world stresses to fall away as I drove the winding roads through the mountains. On the second night in the tepee I told stories to help everyone fall asleep after the highs of the sweat lodge ceremony. I told the tales I knew of Norse gods and Norse Spirituality which had become a favourite subject of mine. As they fell off to sleep one by one, the voice of a Grandmother said, 'You are our storyteller.' This resonated so deep within me: a storyteller! Yes, that's what I wanted to be!

Between 1998 and 2002 I did over 44 sweat lodges, learned how to honour all of creation, became apprenticed to the lodge site, became a Pipe Carrier and learned much from many elders. Yet I never visited the USA! Some people may find that odd but the way I see it is that you don't have to visit Tibet to be a Buddhist, or visit India to be a Yogi, or visit China to become a martial arts warrior. The teachings came to me in the form of many wonderful elders either visiting to pass on knowledge, those who stayed in Europe or those I followed via the joy that is the internet. I visited a few lodge sites in the UK and even helped set up a new one in the borders of Scotland. It was a time where the knowledge was there if you asked in an honourable way. Some elders who came were chastised by tribal leaders who didn't want the teachings shared or watered down. They called people like me 'apples' - red on the outside but white inside. But most of the elders saw it as a time to take these precious teachings about Great Spirit to the Rainbow people as the teachings themselves foretold the time of the Rainbow people who would go forth with the indigenous peoples to fight for the earth. Look at the demonstrations recently at Standing Rock where indigenous people, The Water Protectors, were flanked and supported by people from all over the world. I would have been there had I been younger and fitter. But all I could do was be a supportive keyboard warrior which frustrated me so much. I have had many Native American past lives. My guide is Lakota. I felt I knew the spirituality and culture from the moment I said my first Native American prayer. At one point a Native American elder asked me to come to the USA and go into the reservation schools to show some of the young people how to honour the Ways. She felt that I followed the teachings far more closely than some of the People themselves. So I feel I deserve to be taken seriously because I am committed to my path. I walk my talk. I couldn't live any other way.

I rarely came across any Rainbow person who didn't feel honoured to be learning and didn't do their best to walk their talk. The only person who disappointed me was actually a Native American who came to the UK following success of his book. I had been taught how to prepare for sweat lodges. It started on the Friday night with chants and introductions and the focus of the sweat lodge e.g. whether that be earth healing, personal intentions or honouring of season. There was no alcohol allowed or anything else that could alter the mind. A good sleep was necessary before a good few hours of communal work building the lodge, chopping wood for the fire, clearing the way for the alter while being checked by the Pourer of the sweat lodge that you were indeed fit and well enough in body, mind and soul to actually participate. (No cigarettes were allowed around the Grandfather Fire unless they were natural tobacco and had no tips on them. Even then, tobacco was seen as a sacred herb and not a relaxant.) Then there was a break again to focus on the meaning of the event and being told to drink more and more water. Then it was smudging and purifying time before prayers and chants before even entering the lodge. Then the four rounds of sweats and the huge spiritual experience that was lodge. There would be enough apprentices to look after new people or console or celebrate if it was a family lodge. Then there would be a big feast with plenty of food and juice to drink. Then there was time to sit with an elder or an apprentice to chat about your lodge experience and have them explained to you if you needed that help. Then bed and the deepest sleep with dreams, all of which could again be discussed with people who could help or just listen. There would be a second sweat on the Sunday if anyone wanted it. Sometimes this was time for healing or simply when you wished to feel the closeness of Spirit again. Then there was a cleansing and closing down time and the lodge site was cleaned and tidied and left ready for the next time or dismantled if it wasn't to be permanent. The whole weekend was used and everything had a reason, a teaching and a potential to push yourself out of your comfort zone. No one would be allowed in lodge who wasn't ready for it or medically fit for it.

So by the time I was asked to help prepare the lodge site for this travelling elder I was skilled in the things needed to set up a lodge and, as an apprentice, was skilled at knowing how to help new people prepare for what is mostly an amazing experience. So I found it odd when I was told to simply turn up on the Saturday morning to start preparing the sweat lodge. When I arrived at the site the elder was at the appropriate place and starting the Grandfather Fire. He asked through a helper if I would get the people ready for lodge who would be arriving at eleven a.m. with sweat lodge starting at midday. Alarm bells went off in my head. Hadn't the people been here the previous evening to prepare? No. They arrived in dribs and drabs, most had never partaken in a spiritual sweat before and certainly most had no real understanding of what was about to happen. I explained as much as I could. I asked the elder if he wished me to smudge the people and he said, 'No, don't bother with that.' I was horrified. Not only were the people going into a spiritual ceremony unprepared but they were going in without being cleansed. At that point, I told the group that I wouldn't be doing sweat lodge with this elder because of his lack of attention to teachings and I turned my back and walked away. Should I have done this? It was the only way I could remain calm and not disrespect him in front of people. I was horrified at how little he was going to teach people. It was basically arrive, do lodge, have tea and biscuits, have a talking circle and go home all within six hours. I was so disappointed because I had enjoyed this elder's book and was looking forward to meeting him. But he had been corrupted and it was clear that he was only doing it for the money.

Standing Trees Lodge was precious to me. I met some of the most important people in my life there. I gained so much in working with the teachings, exploring how they could run beside a Scottish Culture. When that part of my life came to an end in 2002 I was devastated. Yet the years that followed proved even more enlightening as I was forced to forge ahead with further learning but without an elder to teach me. And in the years ahead, I became an elder myself.

13

Standing Trees Medicine Lodge was not just important for my spiritual development. It also provided me with my spiritual family who are part of my life now. The people I met there were varied and came from all walks of life. They enriched me beyond belief and I will forever be grateful to them. Some were past life links that the universe reconnected me with to help me become the person I needed to be. My first husband said that meeting my Native American elder and following my spiritual path actually killed our marriage. In a way he was right but our marriage was past its sell by date and in its death throws - Standing Trees simply gave me the self-belief and confidence to say enough was enough. The people who became friends saw how unhappy I was and supported me. The elders who visited to give us teachings and do sweat lodge showed me I was worth more than this. The connection with Great Spirit set a flame alight in me that would never die and it would encourage me to stand in my own Power. My husband said I had changed as a person and this was indeed true. The other side of the coin was that he hadn't.

One of the most important connections for me was a man called Malcolm who I met at the first ever Talking Circle at the Autumn Equinox. I wasn't sure if I liked him at first as he was a bit standoffish and superior. By the end of the weekend though, we were friends. We found so much to talk about and I felt I could be very honest with him about what was going on in my life. He was a good advice giver and I liked his sense of humour. On the second morning we sat near a cairn and put the world to right. In the weeks that followed Malcolm became part of my life and I felt I had a brilliant big brother. I went to

Aberdeen in my worn out banger of a car and he came down south in his motorbike. He visited the premises in Quarry Street for a Halloween party and all the women wanted to know who he was and what our connection was. I think they were stunned when I said he was a brilliant friend and nothing more because right from the beginning we both felt just a beautiful supportive platonic relationship. It was like having my big brother Robert back from Australia and it felt great to have someone so strong by my side. My daughters adored Malcolm and he quickly became their surrogate uncle. He gave them freedom and guidance and love and pocket money! The more we learned spiritually the closer we grew. We shared spiritual journeys and a love of red wine.

Malcolm was a giver. He enjoyed seeing me and my daughters happy. He was generous with his love, time, knowledge and sometimes, when we needed it, money. It felt like someone had given me a strong tree to support me when I needed a rest or a break from worry. It is twenty years since we first met and such a lot of my happy memories have a Malcolm in them! I will love him till the day I die and beyond. To have just him in my life would have been a gift but he also brought me a sister and nieces! Not long into our friendship he asked me and the girls to come up north and meet his new partner, Sooz. I was worried I wouldn't like her and she was worried that she wouldn't get on with me. We needn't have worried! We first became friends and my daughters became friends with her daughters. We seemed to have a way of knowing what the other needed and made sure that we were there for one another. I am sure Malcolm was relieved.

In the years that followed Sooz and I became so close and had so much love for one another. We were so very different in many ways but complemented one another. I don't get her love of Disney songs and she doesn't get my love for Level 42. I am one for blasting out what I feel when I feel it and Sooz bottles things up. My Weegie versus her Doric sometimes causes misunderstanding and great hilarity! Who would have thought that there would be a big difference simply with the word 'fine'? But our friendship just grew and intensified with every year. We seemed to have a deep trust that we would always have the other's back. I thought very long and deep but in 2008 I asked Sooz to become my sister via a 'Making of Relatives' Native American ceremony. This is a blood ceremony and connects two people as blood family. I was ever so relieved when she said yes. We worked towards our ceremony asking ourselves what it would mean to be sisters in every way and when we were ready we had our ceremony. It was beautiful. Our men cast the circle and stood protectively. Our children held a direction each and said their words. Then Sooz and I took our sister vows and we all had a big party and feast. On that day I gained a sister and two brilliant nieces, Becca and Lauren. Jennifer and Jill gained a mad auntie and two cousins who continue to enhance their lives to this day. My husband Jim got a loving sister in law and nieces. And Malcolm who was and is my surrogate brother also became my brother in law! The connection with Malcolm through Standing Trees Medicine Lodge brought me my spiritual family who love and support me to this day.

Other people connected with Standing Trees had a deep effect on me too. There was a man who showed me the meaning of unconditional love and helped me feel lovable and important when I was simply feeling wrecked. He prepared me for the intense love of my life who was still in my future. The couple who hosted the lodge site and the older women partners showed me what balanced and equal relationships looked like. The first Grandmother elder of our community showed me how to be a spiritual Grandmother and what was expected of the role. The children who roamed free without a worry over traffic or the bogeyman showed me how to recapture childlike freedom. The elders who visited and passed on intense teachings and who had very high standards showed me how to walk my talk with discipline and compassion. Through Standing Trees I visited other sweat lodges and spiritual sites with my Pipe and my new sleeping bag, one that wasn't a tenner in the sale. I learned to gather the spiritual tools I needed to become the shaman I had always been.

There was also the joy of understanding why White Storm was my guide and how I was naturally drawn to the Native American way. When I received my first Spirit name 'Quiets the Storm' I was overjoyed with it. Yet the women hugged me hard as they knew that it was a name for someone who was expected to quieten others' storms. In meditation after things calmed down at the ceremony, I sat and White Storm came and sat with me. He said, 'We are both Storm Warriors. Would you like to know my name?' It was then that I realised

'Nindian Boy' was no longer appropriate. Why had I never asked his name before? He seemed to be OK with this oversight and said, 'My name is White Storm.' I remember thinking that it was such a lovely and deep name so I asked him why he had been called White Storm expecting a very deep spiritual answer. He told me that in the Lakota life that he showed himself from, that he had been born in a white storm i.e. a snow storm and therefore had been called White Storm! I remember laughing with him and realising that the gift of my name had opened up a new level of connection between us and I was happy.

Standing Trees also reconnected me with my spirit animal or totem, my panther. She had never really gone away but when she next presented herself she had two cubs with her. I knew then that these two cubs were mirroring my two daughters and that they too had protection and totems of their own. I also became used to animals around me and enjoyed feeding chickens and collecting eggs. I adored the sheep dogs and despised the geese who seemed to chase me every chance they had. I went from growing up in a Glasgow suburb with no real access to wildlife to spending time among it and enjoying it so much. Nature became my drug of choice. I communed with trees and looked for water sprites in the stream and salamanders in the grandfather fire. I learned what leaves you could eat and how to grow herbs. I learned how to waken with the sun and do Pipe prayers before Grandfather Sun was very high in the sky and to sit in harmony and watch the sun go down surrounded by friends, animals and spirits. I did my Vision Quest and received the answers I already knew. I learned how to use a drum to meditate to and to heal with and how to make a medicine bag. I finally let my voice free and chanted with the best of them. I learned how to dig a fire pit and how to construct a mother lodge for sweats. I learned how to pour the lodge itself and look after people in what were to be spiritual ceremonies that would change their lives. I also learned that I had stamina and could use mind over matter techniques when I needed to. I learned that I could push myself way outside of my comfort zone and still survive. In five years I went from being Colette Clairvoyant to Quiets the Storm, the shaman who felt like a warrior when it came to magick and healing and the environment. I knew the love of good people who never bothered whether I had my mascara on or not and preferred me covered in sweat and mud anyway! My first husband was right - I had changed and I was never going back!

What happens in sweat lodge stays in sweat lodge. It is never discussed unless with an elder or someone who was present and wants to listen. To me it will always be the most intense connection with not only the higher beings but also myself. It isn't easy and is not for everyone but if you feel drawn to it I suggest you find a good spiritual place that offers sweat lodge and make inquiries. I don't know if I will do any more sweats. I don't feel my health is good enough now. I would be a danger to myself and a danger to others but I have done so many and have such special memories of them, that I am contented and proud to have done them. I try to walk in beauty, balance and harmony every day and to be available to help people spiritually. I now live in a wee cottage with nature all around me and as I sit here writing this there is a thunderstorm with lightening so I will finish and go stand in the rain and enjoy the cleansing.

Although Standing Trees Medicine Lodge was a place of learning it was also a place of great fun and humour. I look back and see such fun and laughter and sometimes cringe at some of my mistakes. My first sweat lodge was an intense experience. I wasn't very confident in my body so I turned up in a one piece black swimsuit with shorts and a tee shirt on top. I looked really out of place as most other people had either bikinis on or were naked underneath their towels. I also had my earrings in and my necklace on even though I had been advised that this was not a good idea. That first blast of steam from the red hot stones hit me like a wall of fire. My tee shirt melded itself to my swimsuit which melded itself to my skin. Within minutes my shorts were soaked in sweat and I was so very uncomfortable. I wanted out so badly but was not going to be defeated. Soon the prayers and chants lifted me and I managed to keep going. I was very uncomfortable but it was about to become worse - my ear lobes seemed to be on fire! And my chest felt like a hot stone was burning through it. This was because my jewellery had become so hot it was burning me. This was another distraction that I didn't need in this spiritual place. When the door was opened after the first round to let a breeze in before more hot stones were brought in I quickly took all my jewellery off. I noticed that the women in bikinis and men in shorts were all done in already like me.

Yet those sensible souls who had come in in a towel and gently dropped it when the door closed and the lodge was completely dark, well, they were doing just fine.

I literally crawled out of my first sweat lodge and collapsed onto the wet grass. I felt elated and completely spent. I resolved to never, ever go into a sweat with a swimsuit and tee shirt and shorts on again. The next sweat lodge weekend saw me enter lodge with a tee shirt and knickers on. The overall result was still agony but I was still so unconfident in my body that I couldn't strip off. The most annoying thing was that absolutely no one was interested in how I looked. It was a spiritual gathering of many ages and shapes and sizes who were all focused on having a spiritual cleansing with like-minded people. I was silly to be bothered at all. The nakedness wasn't overt at all anyway. Towels were simply dropped when the sweat lodge started and it was dark. Over the next few months I discarded my tee shirt and went in just in pants under my towel. It was such a relief not to have heavy cotton clothes clinging to me for four hours. Think of an elongated sauna with clothes on and multiply it by a hundred and you will come close to my discomfort. I held on to my pants for at least my first year of sweat lodge then one day I had enough. I went in naked under my towel and had the best lodge ever apart from one thing. As I sat on the good grass in the sweat lodge a twig lodged itself in my buttock! It was as though nature was having a laugh! I finally had the courage to take my pants off and Mother Nature took the opportunity to have a wee stab at me. I still have the mark!

Standing Trees showed me how little I actually knew of the world of nature or life outside of a suburb. I didn't know how to make a fire and light it without a lighter. I didn't know how to work the smoke flaps of the tepee and nearly asphyxiated myself. My arms weren't strong and moving the poles to open the smoke flaps was almost too much for me. They were heavy and I was weak. So I resolved that I would become more physically fit. I had dislocated my knee over seventeen times so I was never going to be the strongest but I wanted to be able to cut wood and carry it to the lodge site, to have control of the tepee, to be able to endure longer sweats and to be able to walk further. I learned to use a saw and an axe to cut wood. The grandfather fire for the sweat lodge weekends burned so much wood and we literally cut it the morning before we entered. After a few years I would be teaching new people to cut wood and help them keep going when their arms were feeling like lead. I had two ways of doing this. The first was very spiritual. I got them to join in with a power chant and we got a good rhythm going with the double handled saw. The second wasn't so spiritual and was for the point where we were too tired to chant. I used to say that the logs were long and their circumference was about the size of a supermodels waist! So, without bad intent, we set about chopping up super models, cutting them down to size while laughing at our own normal bodies and waist sizes.

Standing Trees Medicine Lodge will always be such a part of me. I would go as far as to say it made me who I am today. It provided me with skills, both spiritual and practical, friends and eventually family, teachings, affirmations of who I was and ultimately the strength to walk my talk and be my authentic self.

.

14

By summer of 2001 I had officially separated from my husband, Hamilton Psychic Forum was no more and my time at Standing Trees Medicine Lodge was over. I had a brilliant fortieth birthday party with all my friends and family there and had started to do my clairvoyant readings from home. I had very mixed emotions about this - I had been used to having premises and had hoped always to have them so I felt a bit humiliated. Yet there was also a great degree of freedom and it meant I was always there for my daughters. The three of us settled into a routine where I worked two days a week and two evenings. On the evenings they would have their dinner, hoover and tidy while I set up my cards and meditated and then they disappeared to their rooms with snacks and the odd friend. Or went outside to play knowing I was accessible through the back door at any time. I was still doing events to try to pay the forum debts off and the occasional house party. I was busy and continually stressed over money. I was relieved not to have to travel back and forth to work and enjoyed having my bedroom to myself without male presence. I had it painted white and went very girly with my bed linen and curtains. I had so many good friends who were cheerleaders when I was low. Plus, I loved my work. I had worried that clients wouldn't follow me from Hamilton in South Lanarkshire to Chapelhall in North Lanarkshire but I don't think I lost any regulars at all. I remember it being a time of sunshine, wine, good conversation and further spiritual development.

One of the funniest things that happened after I started working from home concerned a nosy neighbour from across the road. This neighbour always knew the gossip of the estate and I avoided her as I don't enjoy gossip or folk who take delight in putting others down. I have been very lucky in my profession that I read for quite a high proportion of men, mainly through business or spiritual path-working consultations. I enjoy a healthy mix of genders, 'normal' people, posh people, celebrities, politicians and sports people. It just so happened that on the first week I worked from home, six of my clients in a row were businessmen with fancy cars who zoomed up, parked outside my door, came in for an hour and then zoomed away again! I had noticed as I watched for them arriving that my nosy neighbour's curtain twitched every time someone arrived and she blatantly glared at me from across the road. I was perturbed. I had lived here for two years and had never seen her so interested before. Later on that week I was in the garden and she came over and asked me if I was not working anymore. I replied that yes I was but I was working from home now rather than out of a premises. She asked me if I enjoyed my work with all the men who came and I said yes that I really enjoyed it. I felt very uncomfortable and caught in her headlights. It wasn't until she said that it was a quiet cul-de-sac and that she was aware of the men coming in cars that it dawned on me that she thought I was 'entertaining' men at home! I burst out laughing and made the point of saying, 'Yes, it is nice to have a good percentage of men who come for psychic readings and don't some of my businessmen have amazing cars?' She immediately turned bright red when she realised her mistake. I never really heard much from her after that.

One of the businessmen who came to visit me at my home was quite rude. He adored his reading but on his way out he looked round my living room and said, 'I have noticed that you people never seem to have very much, do you?' I asked him what he meant by 'you people' and also what he meant by 'very much'. He intimated that he meant 'clairvoyants and fortune tellers' and that he meant that we never had good furniture or evidence of wealth. I was horrified at this because we were in my detached new build home which was lovely. I have always been frugal and love up cycling things. But at this time I was also struggling to pay off the Forum debt and look after two children. My sofa and chairs were about ten years old and my wicker cabinet had been rescued from the Forum. What he saw was an old couch and an inexpensive cabinet. What I saw was all I needed decorated with boho stuff, with shamanic art on the walls and crystals in most nooks and crannies. I saw a home filled with love and a comfortable space to live and live well. When I looked back at him it wasn't with shame but with pity. He judged my life by his standards and found it lacking. Yet, when I judged my life by my standards I found it full, abundant and happy.

I was finding myself emotionally discarding old feelings of low self-esteem and low self-worth when it came to men. I had dated a younger man, had a few blind dates set up by friends and been told by a female friend who was gay that she really loved me and wished us to be closer. This came as a shock to me as although I have many gay and homosexual friends, I am probably one of the most heterosexual women I know. I love and connect with people at a soul level so gender isn't important to me where unconditional love is concerned. I do find the female form the more beautiful in aesthetic terms to look at. But as far as sexual attraction goes I am very much a heterosexual woman who lusts after Daniel Craig and Ross Poldark. But it was nice to be asked! By the winter of 2001 I was a bit fed up with the dating scene as I wasn't really meeting anyone special or as spiritual as I needed. I wasn't lonely as such as I was still very busy and in recovery from my marriage breakdown but I was missing the closeness of having a partner, albeit I didn't want one who would interfere with my new life. I had a child-free weekend while my daughters were staying with their dad and on the Friday night I opened a nice bottle of wine (or was it a box?) and proceeded to get a wee bit drunk. I had no real plans for the weekend apart from cleaning the house and listening to music. I love music and listened to it a lot after my marriage breakup. In fact one weekend when I was a bit low and the girls were with me they gave me an insight into how children see things. I had been feeling a bit overwhelmed by everything that had happened and it was a Saturday night and my daughters age 13 and 8 were going up to bed. They came to me and said, 'Mum, why don't you have a Toni Braxton night tonight and you will feel so much better in the morning.' I was bemused and asked what a Toni Braxton night was? The wee one said, 'Well it is the nights where we go to bed and you open some wine and then put on Toni Braxton's song 'Unbreak My Heart' and sing along a few times. Then more sad music comes on and you go to bed. And in the morning you feel great and all happy again.' I had to laugh. I had gotten through my sadness by the 'wine and music' method but hadn't thought my daughters were so aware of it. It was time to move on!

So that Friday night I decided to talk to the Universe about my needs for a perfect man. This was done under the influence of wine and was very much tongue in cheek as White Storm watched and laughed. It went a little like this and please don't judge me for being dishonourable to the Universe or Spirit.

'Okay Universe, I need to find the perfect man and I know what I want so come close and listen in because I need you to know what I want! First he needs to have nice eyes, as I like nice eyes on a man! Oh and nice arms…I like nice toned arms! Oh and most important he needs to be spiritual! I need someone who understands who I am and need to be. Not that he will be living with me or anything. No I don't want a live in partner! I want someone to have fun with and to support me! Oh, it would be nice too if he had a science background like me as I do enjoy talking about science as well as paranormal. Can you do that Universe? Oh please do. Oh and…I don't want him to have children as if it does become more then step children can be tough and 'blended ' families are hard going. So no children please? Oh and music…he needs to like David Grey as the White Ladder CD is all I am playing just now! Okay, okay…that's my 'cosmic order' so off you go and manifest me my Mr Perfect partner!'

After my rant I realised that I had drank quite a lot of wine and White Storm was laughing at me so I knew I had not offended anyone. Yet, White Storm had that little mischievous glint in his eye that normally meant either trouble ahead or a big life lesson.

I had some food and settled down to go on AOL and surf the internet. I checked my emails and there was one from a businessman who had a few proposals about my psychic fayres and asked to talk to me about them. I replied to the email that I didn't have premises anymore and was doing events. He replied he knew that and maybe had some options for me. We ended up taking on AOL messenger about business and he had some ideas that sounded interesting. To cut a long story short I agreed to meet him for a drink the next day at a nice pub. We had chatted for about two hours and I felt a little bit of a connection so decided that maybe business could connect me with my Mr Perfect so why not give it a chance. I was interested to see this new man the next day and also a little nervous. I liked his outlook on business practices as he had told me that he too had a science background although his business was very different now. We had also talked about some spiritual views we both firmly believed in. Could the Universe be working this quickly to bring me Mr Perfect? Spiritual - tick. Background in science - tick.

So I walked into the pub and saw him right away. I knew it was him. He had spectacular blue eyes and had his shirt sleeves rolled up showing very toned and tanned arms. Tick. Tick. He bought me a drink and we set about talking business mixed with personal details. I talked about my daughters and he said he didn't have children. Tick! By this time I though the Universe was playing a very surreal joke or providing me with a lesson. After we realised that our businesses didn't actually align in future direction, he said, let's just relax and enjoy what is left of the day. He said he would put some music on the jukebox. As he walked back one of my favourite David Grey songs came on. He said, 'I love David Grey. Do you like him?' and I nearly choked on my drink. Tick! So this man ticked every box or demand from my drunken wish the previous night. Every single one of them. Yet I felt no real spark and no real wish to see him another time. We had a drink and I got my taxi home. The house was empty and I had time to sit silently and think on what had happened. This man had ticked every box that I wanted ticked for my perfect man yet he didn't do anything for me. There was no spark. I asked White Storm what this was all about. He said it showed me the power of my magickal intent and to let it serve as a warning before I do anything. He also said that it was a lesson on what I thought I wanted. He said that when my perfect match came he wouldn't fulfil all of my boxes but it wouldn't matter as he would be perfect for me and me for him. I had a wee cry. I learned a big lesson about the power of magick and also was told that my perfect partner was still ahead of me, but would eventually come. After that I simply enjoyed a few dates but mainly hung out with friends and family and enjoyed all the love around me. Isn't magick wonderful?

The Universe added new spiritual friends to replace the Standing Trees friends while my spiritual connection with Malcolm and Sooz blossomed into a lovely family unit. I connected with a brilliant friend Stevie through connection to his spirit guide and his spectacular artwork is in most rooms of my house . His most recent one of recycled railway wood surrounding a silver thistle takes pride of place above my fireplace. Stevie brings laughter wherever he goes. We bonded through spirituality but in the years that followed, with our views on Scottish independence. In my grandmother years I have become very political. I also dated a lovely man called Steven who also brought laughter into our lives. But it was not meant to be as my life partner. I remember this time as one of spiritual friendships, sunshine, growth for my daughters and hard work for me.

I remember in the autumn of 2002, on a visit to Aberdeen, discussing with Malcolm that I was ready for a new partner, one who would nurture me and love my daughters. He said he knew that the person would be there for me but maybe it would be a while and I needed to be patient. Patience has never been a strong point when I set my heart on something. When I returned home I went into a deep meditation and asked my guide via my tarot, just when my soul mate would turn up if left to the natural flow of things. I also remembered the psychic Leandra telling me I would marry twice and both would be astrological fire signs. My first husband was an Aries. Again the cards showed that this man was definitely there for me but it might take about 4 years. I thought 'stuff that! I want him here sooner' and prepared to do the magick to bring him here quicker. I was aware that there can always be consequences in doing this but was prepared to take the risk.

I thought deeply on how to compose my intent. It had to be specific enough to only bring my soul connection towards me and not a progression of 'nearly Mr Rights'. So after a full night's meditation I had gathered the items I needed for my intent and also the words I would use to make this so. I figured out that I would never be likely to marry again but since Leandra had seen two marriages I decided to lay down the words 'bring me the man whose name I will take in marriage.' That seemed to me like a cast iron expression of my will. It had to be the man whose name I would take if I *were* to marry again. The spell felt intense and I felt invigorated after doing it. This was going to work. I just knew it. Three weeks later I met a nice man. He was gentle, funny and kind. He was called Jim Brown and I liked him a lot. The girls found him quite likable and we dated a little but in my heart I felt that this wasn't right. Something was very right about him but the deep spiritual connection I expected of a soul mate just wasn't there. We parted amicably and with a sense of relief as we both knew it wasn't what we wanted. I was confused because I really felt I connected to something about this Jim Brown and was sure my magick had brought him towards me.

I had met a new friend many months previously on an alternative spirituality site online and we generally chatted and put the world to right. Bob was intense about his magickal practices and also loved music so it wasn't long before he invited me to his home in the central belt for some veggie food and to hear some of his music live. The first time Bob opened the door to me I felt that he was looking behind me which was odd. A few months later he would tell me that when he opened the door to me he saw a premonition of not just me at his door but me and one of his best friends, who had his arm around me. This was after he had made it his priority to introduce us, which he did. He said that I would like his friend Jim who now lived in Ireland but was due a visit to Scotland. He said he followed a shamanic path like me. Bob, being a more High Magick person, referred to this as 'dead animal on a stick' magick which I found quite funny but I didn't really take in much about his friend. But matchmaker Bob wasn't to be outdone. He managed to introduce us a few months later. This was out of blue and a few weeks after I had let 'Jim Brown' from my spell go and almost forgotten about it. When I met Bob's friend Jim there was just a kind of click. It was like going home. We talked all night about spirituality and life and loves and failures. The weirdest thing happened too. He was dressed in jeans and had a bandanna on. He had a long pony tail but was bald above it. He wore a fringed jacket and looked just like an old hippy! I immediately flashed back to the feelings I felt when I was a teenager in Rutherglen when the gardener came to cut my mum's grass and I felt such an amount of love. That gardener who confused the life out of me due to intensity of feelings was the image of Jim. Or Jim was the image of him. I felt confused again to feel those intense feelings. By the end of the night Jim and I had acknowledged that there was something stirring. He wanted to send me a gift of some oils that I was having difficulty finding and in turn I wanted to send him some feathers I knew he would like. But I didn't even know his surname? I gasped when he said, 'It is Brown. Jim Brown.' So the Universe had sent me the correct Jim Brown, only after sending the wrong Jim Brown, which I see as a kind of test. Would I be prepared to let go of something OK in order to find something amazing? I was and I did. I still laugh when I remember my spell which I thought was invincible,

'Bring me the person whose name I will take in marriage.' It brought me two Jim Browns, but only one of them was the right one.

.

INTERLUDE

DURGA

My Native American path was a very happy one for me. It allowed me to be who I truly needed to be. It also was a path that accepted many supernatural beings all connected and part of the creator. I still had a love of Jesus as a god but not as the only god. I studied Norse spirituality and had devotions on and off to the Norse deities. I connected strongly with Frigga and Tyr. In the late 2000s I found myself drawn to Hindu deities but in a very gentle way because some of my friends were Hindu and I enjoyed their festivals and my celebrations with them. I loved the colours and dancing and food and sheer joy of these times. Many of my clients were also Hindu so I felt very grateful for my connection.

Goddess Lakshmi was a deity that I felt very comfortable with. She seemed to reflect parts of me that I knew and understood. I always had a fascination with the Elephant God Ganeesh as my dad had served in India and loved the people and the elephants. By 2008, I was following an intense Native American spirituality with prayers and ceremonies simply a part of my life. Yet I also felt drawn to Lakshmi as a deity to whom I could do prayer and ritual.

One night early in 2009 Jim and I were at home looking at some spiritual work we wished to do, when we both felt a huge presence enter the room. Jim felt dizzy and knew that the being was behind him. I felt I had stopped breathing. And there, manifesting in our work room, was Ganeesh, the elephant headed god. I had never felt anything like this in my life. Jim said I was glued to my chair and couldn't move.

119

I felt elated and joyful but aware that there was a message for us from this amazing god. Ganeesh was speaking in Hindi so the best I could do was try to write it down phonetically. Once this was done, I bowed my head and Jim followed and I felt tears run from my eyes. Then Ganeesh was gone. We sat in silence for a while, aware of the enormity of what had happened.

The next day I sent the words from Ganeesh to one of my Hindu friends who had her father, a beautiful, spiritual man, translate them as best he could. There were two messages. One said that we should honour Ganeesh more and place gifts at his feet. The other was a command to give more to charity as we were blessed in this life and needed to help those who weren't. We resolved to do both in honour of our special visitor. Two days later, a wonderful client and friend phoned and said to Jim that she had a charity event coming up and would I care to offer readings to the party goers while money auctions and entertainments were going ahead in the main hall. I remembered Ganeesh's words and told Jim to say yes right away. It was only after he came off the phone I realised that we didn't know what the charity was. So we phoned back and were told that it was a huge night to raise funds for Age Concern India! It just felt right and I was happy to be part of it a few weeks later. The event itself was very successful in raising money for both Age Concern India and UK. I met some very interesting people including a wonderful man who would become a friend. I also purchased Ganeesh statues and made regular offerings of sweets and money.

So my connection with the Hindu deities would continue. Jim connected with Hannuman, the Monkey God, and enjoyed time learning from him. I continued to offer devotions to Lakshmi and Ganeesh while following my Native American path. It didn't feel odd as it all comes from Source or Creator and how we connect with this is very personal. But it was about to get serious and blow my mind!

After Blessed Bee, our shop, closed Jim felt depressed and distraught. His dream of helping folk navigate life via spirituality had ended and he felt redundant. Even though he was still running his website shop, he missed the connection with real people. He also was diagnosed with spinal arthritis and was in a lot of pain. His low mood was very difficult at a time that my daughters were at important stages in their education. This alienated them from him and he felt left out and as though we didn't need him. I had started to go through menopause. The energy in the house was bad. I sadly began to feel like my soul mate was becoming a stranger though I still loved him intensely. I am sure he felt the same. We tried as best we could but by March 2010 we couldn't see a way forward and sadly, he left. I was distraught as were my girls who saw how upset I was. Jim stayed with some friends in Stirling and I proceeded to adapt to my work and readings without Jim there in the background looking after me. My daughters stepped in to help let clients in and out and we never really said much to anyone apart from close family. Jim needed time and I had to keep going so that we didn't go under financially.

I had the full support of my spiritual family and I knew Jim was being well looked after by his friends. One of the lovely supports was my old friend John Doyle who re-appeared in my life bringing his lovely wife Michele. A few months earlier he had turned up at my door by mistake looking for someone else. I looked at him and he looked at me and said, 'Colette Ferrie?' And I said, 'John Doyle?' and after thirty years my childhood friend was back. He had been living in the same village as us and we never knew. John and Michele were always available when I needed a coffee and someone to talk to. I felt alone and missed Jim terribly but my girls had exams and I knew I had to pull it together for them. But I was lost. Jim and I had met up and knew we still loved one another but still couldn't see a way forward. I knew I had to do something as being in limbo was killing me but I knew it would be hard. I knew that I needed to do a ritual to Goddess Lakshmi to bring me back stability but to do it I knew I had to accept whatever outcome was correct, even if that meant I never saw Jim again. I knew I needed to offer her my total trust to sort it out and to accept the future she presented. My heart hurt but I knew it was the only way.

So I gathered my thoughts and prepared for the ritual of my life. I gathered offerings to Lakshmi including a piece of gold jewellery that Jim had given me. I knew I would never be able to wear it again but I would have sold my granny by this point. I gathered special flowers and magickal essences and put them all together in my offering bag. Then I prepared myself by cleansing and put on some beautiful clothes and perfume and make up. I wanted to stand proud and strong in front of

Goddess. The previous night I had been sad because I had cleaned out the room upstairs that I had used as a reading room before I had moved it downstairs to answer the door to clients when Jim wasn't there during the day. It had no furniture now and was hoovered and dusted to within an inch of its life. It was symbolic of the emptiness I felt. I didn't know what I would use it for and closed the door sadly on it; like I was going to close the door on the marriage if that's what my Goddess showed was right for all concerned.

I was about to go downstairs to my new reading and devotional room with my offerings and my ritual words in my head when I felt a very impressive energy in the air. The room became amber and smelt of exotic flowers and I felt my head spin. I felt that Lakshmi was manifesting but when I looked it was Goddess Durga herself who appeared. I thought I would faint. She said if I was ready to do what I said that she would take my burden and give me the right outcome. I answered yes. She indicated that my offering pouch was missing something and told me it was in the other room, across the hall, my old reading room. I opened the door slowly wondering what it could be as I had left nothing in the room. It was starkly empty. Yet when I looked I saw the largest queen bee lying on the carpet. I wasn't sure if she was dead or alive so I approached with care. But she was dead, perfect but dead. Her wings were perfect and crystallised like she had died in flight. I picked her up and put her in my offering bag. There was no way she was there when I had shut the room up the previous night. And then I broke my heart and did the most powerful ritual of my life. I gave up total control which is hard for a Taurus. I gave my burdens to Durga and resolved to accept whatever came next for Jim and I, knowing it would be for the best even if I didn't like it. I felt a huge weight lifted from me and I cried a river.

I buried the hessian offering bag complete with gold and magickal herbs in a planter that I was growing Echinacea flowers in. Then I set about getting on with life. The girls sat their exams. Jim worked on what he needed to. I realised that if I truly had to, I could manage on my own with my daughters, as we had before Jim came. I just didn't want to. And Jim and I realised that we simply needed to make it work. He came back four months later and we had family counselling which gave the girls a chance to have their say and be understood. It wasn't easy but what was a simple truce, in time, has led to us becoming a very happy family with so much love for one another.

After Jim came home I decided it was time to bury the offering pouch in the back garden rather than in a patio pot. The Echinacea flowers hadn't done very well. It was autumn and time for clearing up. When I dug down I couldn't find anything. So I turned the pot upside down. The pouch had gone. I was shocked as even if the hessian had disintegrated in four months, surely the gold would still be there? Nothing. It had all simply disappeared! Including the precious queen bee. I told my Hindu friends about this months later. They said that the bees were precious to Durga and considered her companions. I totally believe that Durga gifted me the queen bee for my ritual then took her back when all was done and well. Namaste Durga!

So I have been devoted to Durga ever since and Jim and I have never looked back. We have valued the lesson in a way because we know what we nearly lost. I pray to Durga and Great Spirit. I honour the earth and the shamanic way of the Native Americans and I am devoted to Durga. I celebrate the turning seasons and Navratri, Durga's festival, every year. I say prayers that start with 'Hear me Great Spirit' or 'Hear me Durga' depending on how I feel and both ways are part of my life.

Sometimes this caused me to feel a little uncomfortable but I did it anyway. I asked for guidance and not to offend either tradition. One day while I was deep in meditation I saw Durga walking towards me with my spirit guide White Storm. They walked in harmony, in a quiet sort of understanding, a goddess and a higher guide. I asked them what was their message. White Storm said, 'Don't worry about having a foot in each way. Don't worry or feel torn. Because people like you who know more than one way and can show how to walk like this will be necessary to teach others.' And then they disappeared. I was overjoyed. I felt I had been given permission to live my life and walk my talk. I have never been as contented spiritually as I am now. It feels wonderful.

.

15

The real Jim Brown left his job, friends and family in Ireland within four month of us meeting. We did the distance relationship thing and he came over at Christmas to meet my daughters. This went incredibly well and the following February he came here for good. This was a huge risk for both of us but it felt right. The universe had provided a very interesting option for us both and we felt that we should give it a go. My friend and client Carol had a hairdressers and beauty salon in Strathaven, a wee town that my mum and dad had always taken me to for day out in the summer. It was quaint, pretty and busy in the summer. She had a kind of extension to her salon with its own door that had been used by a Reiki healer but was now empty. She said that when she first came into the premises she had a vision of it decorated with dream-catchers and Native American art and thought of me. She asked me if I would like it as premises for my readings. Initially I had said no because I didn't feel up to employing a secretary or being responsible for a shop after the demise of the Forum. But with Jim on board the proposition looked very different. He had always wanted to be able to have a pagan shop where he could make incenses and provide stock and advice. The more we thought and talked about it, the more of an answer it became to us. So Jim left his upholstery career behind and came to Scotland and we opened Blessed Bee.

The only problem was that we had limited finances and I wasn't willing to divert household cash to the business as I had done in the Forum. So we asked for friends and family to help with stock. One of my spirit sisters from Standing Tree Medicine Lodge provided authentic dream catchers as sale or return and they looked amazing hanging around the shop. People were amazed by them but also the price because they were totally authentic and not like the £3.99 ones from What Every Woman Wants! The feathers, the stones, the weaving were all so stunning. They were works of art. We felt we were educating people about the difference between authentic and mass produced. We also had Native American jewellery and smudge sticks and feather fans. We spent money on a selection of crystals and incense sticks. We met a beautiful woman called Hazel through a friend who made crystal jewellery and she too gave stock on a sale or return basis. Jim made all the shelves himself and painted the rooms. I stayed at home and did my readings as he worked 12 hour shifts getting the place ready to open at the spring equinox. The place looked lovely but a wee bit under stocked. My reading room was a delightful sage green colour and when I moved my bits and bobs in it felt great. Now all we had to do was hope the stock sold but more importantly that my ever loyal clients would follow me away from North Lanarkshire back to South Lanarkshire to a town with bad transport links and bad parking. Once again, they never let me down. I have often said that I have had the best clients in the world and the fact that they just followed me wherever I went is testament to that.

Jim was in his element. He replaced his jeans and bandanna for a smart black suit and got to know my clients. We were like a tag team. I would do their reading then suggest a crystal or therapy or even just to talk to Jim about a spiritual issue and then he would take over. We worked hard but it was a joy. We had a lesson early on about not doing anything out with the shop. Carol and her team had been invited to go to a Goldwing motorbike festival in the borders and provide hair, massage, make up and face painting and asked us to come too to provide readings and set up our shop. This meant almost taking all our stock in the car and shutting the shop for five days. We were worried that we would actually lose money when hotels and meals etc. were factored in but were assured by the people running the festival that it was huge and our stock and services would sell. So we packed up and arrived on the Thursday for what ended up being a total fiasco for us and also for Carol and her staff. We had a great time hanging out and drinking wine at night but the festival itself was not something I would ever repeat.

When we arrived on the Friday to set up my 'reading room' it was still being made! There was a kind of stall beside Carol's hair/ beauty area which also still had no running water or door. We were in a huge barn of a place that looked empty and I wondered how people would find us. We were told this was going to be the busiest place all weekend. Jim went to set up our 'shop' in the main sales hall while I waited around to see if my room would be ready even for some bookings in the afternoon. It looked like the paint would be dry and I was found a table and two chairs. I started to decorate the cubicle feeling a sense of dread. Jim came back with coffee for me and told me that our shop stall was right at the back of the main hall surrounded by bike insurance stalls and stalls with bike parts. He was not happy. But we decided to make the most of it because at least my reading space was going to be in a busy part - so we had been told. As I sat down to meditate there was a huge boom and splat noise outside. Then again and again. This horrendous noise was soon joined by a high pitch sound like a dentist's drill. I ventured outside to see that right outside of where I was meant to be doing meaningful clairvoyant and mediumistic readings that there was a pressurized pump machine and a huge array of what looked like electric drills. I had been put beside a craftsman and artist who would spend 4 days inscribing motorbikes with artwork! Basically a tattooist for bikes. And he was going to be busy because he was well known as the best! I could have cried. But it got worse as motorbikes lined up outside all revving engines. Carol went to the organizer right away to get something else sorted for me. She would take over my cubicle and do beard extensions of various colours which would be popular while the guys waited on their bikes being engraved. Poor Carol, she did her best but the stress of what was unfolding and the thought of all the money she could lose was taking its toll. She also felt annoyed for encouraging us to come but had been so kind and helpful and really it was no one's fault apart from maybe the organizers and to be honest I didn't feel they knew what our needs were.

We abandoned ship on the Friday with hope of a new day on the Saturday. The Saturday was still only for bikers who had signed up and were camping but the Sunday was open to the public after a big ride-out for charity. The Monday was back to being for bikers only. We felt that there was a chance to sell some lovely stock and maybe I would have somewhere quiet and secure to read from. On the Saturday morning we arrived and the organizers showed me to where they expected me to do my readings and assured me they had bookings for me. It was a tent! Now those of you who know me know I genuinely hate the 'fortune teller in tent with crystal ball and headscarf and kohl eyeliner' look. The tiny tent set in a field next to a burger van felt like the low spot of my career. One look at Jim's furious face and I decided to make the best of a bad situation. He was raging about my reputation, having been on TV and having business and celebrity clients and them putting me in a tent! I thought he was going to punch the organizer. So I calmed him, swallowed my pride and set up in the tent. My first client came in and immediately we connected and felt that there would be a real good reading that would benefit her. Then the wind became stronger and the tent started to implode! We abandoned it when the first tent peg ripped itself out of the ground. I went to where Jim was sitting like Johnny-No-Pals and had a cry. This was turning into a nightmare.

We sold one dream-catcher and one skull ring on the Saturday. We chatted to lot of people and we knew Carol was busy by the amount of men we saw with multi-coloured beards. Our only hope was that the open day on the Sunday would bring in some much needed sales. It didn't. We learned that bikers spend huge amounts of money on their bikes but very little on anything else. The general public came to see the ride out and then saw a huge barn full of bike parts and paint and polish and went straight home. By three o clock we packed up the car, gave Carol and the girls a hug and started off home so that we could at least open the shop again on the Tuesday. It was a huge lesson. I vowed if I ever saw a Goldwing bike again I would slit its tyres. Later, a biker friend who had a Harley Davidson said, 'Oh never do a Goldwing festival! They are tight with money. Do a Harley festival. We spend money on art and tee shirts and jewellery and love Native American stuff.' Eh, no thanks! Jim and I resolved never ever to move out with the shop again.

The first Christmastime in the shop was successful. People seemed to love our unusual crafts and crystals. Working next door to Carol and her staff was fun and everything was very festive. Jim enjoyed his status as the only male among six women. It was fun and we were doing what we loved. The readings were booked for months in advance. But the January and February were dire with only my readings keeping us going.

Jim realised that pagans don't have much money and tended to make things like incense for themselves. It seemed to be younger goths that were keeping us going and a few folk in Strathaven crossed the street when they saw us coming as though we were Satanists which was so unfair! We didn't care that much though. We were helping people.

Jim became known for his sage advice and down to earth attitude. I was often referred to as 'that spooky woman'. We made a good team and our relationship grew deeper and stronger. We began running shamanic workshops where I taught and Jim drummed the meditations. Jim had played in folk bands and was a wonderful Bodhran drummer. The workshops were well attended and we always felt elated when we had finished one. The shop had good months and bad months but we were happy albeit very tired.

I rarely remember what I say in readings as most of it comes as channelling or quick visions combined with my beloved tarot. This has caused some problems with some clients who believe I should remember what I said to them six months previously and can be quite deflated when I don't. So I sometimes just nod and know that I will see what has happened in the cards anyway. Most people are lovely about it though as was proved to me by an incident in Strathaven. A woman, who I remembered reading for but not the specifics, approached me on the street with a big smile and said,

'Oh Colette, what you said in the reading happened to me!'

Having no clue what I had said but seeing she was smiling, I replied,

'Brilliant. Wonderful. I am pleased!'

Her smile faded quickly and she said,

'No, it wasn't good. I *did* have breast cancer!'

I felt like disappearing into my boots with shame. She was lovely though and explained that in her reading, I had asked her to go for a mammogram as I was worried about a mark I saw in her aura. She said that she had one three months previously and it was clear. But she saw I looked worried and went to clinical centre for another one. This one showed a very fast growing cancer. This was removed and she was having therapy and her prognosis was good. She was so happy that I had picked up on it. I resolved never to pretend I remembered what I had said in a reading again. I should have remembered a similar lesson from my pharmacy days when a man returned to my shop and asked for 'another one of those brilliant bottles that dried it up quickly'. I asked him if it was a particular caught bottle and he laughed and said, 'No, it was for diarrhoea!'

In winter 2003 we were diverted from the Strathaven road due to snow. The 6 mile diversion took us through a village called Blackwood. I remember being annoyed at the delay but as we went through Blackwood I commented how lovely it was and how I would love to live there. I passed a large detached house as I said this and felt a weird pull. Five months later we ended up living in that same house after the fates and my divorce plans moved us on from Chapelhall. I had promised my daughters when I separated from their dad that I would never lose our home in Chapelhall and I worked every hour I could to keep it. But when people part and there is equity to be shared sometimes you can't keep your promises. I felt so sad and simply the worst mum ever.

Yet the move to Blackwood was a blessing in disguise. Jennifer transferred to a new school and with hard work and determination succeeded in getting into Strathclyde University to study History and Politics and teaching. Jill was very shy and went to a very small primary school and then on to a secondary that nurtured her natural talent in English and writing. We were only 6 miles from the shop instead of 15 miles so we spent much less time travelling and more time as a family. The house in Blackwood was lovely and very spacious. It felt very sunny. It was a great house for a party and we hosted many. It was the natural place to hold our wedding party when we married in 2005.

Jim and I had a lovely legal service at Hamilton Town House followed by our hand-fasting in our garden. I went all out and had a white heavy silk dress with Anne Boleyn sleeves and a corseted front. Jim wore a kilt. It was a beautiful day filled with happiness and joy. Our family and friends were there. I walked down the aisle at the civil ceremony to 'Something About You' by Level 42, my favourite band, and down the garden at my hand-fasting to Enigma, Return to Innocence. The band for the night was my nephew Andy and his friends and later on the extra drums and guitars came out and the chants and songs began. The whole day was full of love. I will never forget it. We recently danced to the same Level 42 song at my daughter's wedding celebrating our twelfth anniversary.

We carried on in the shop but Carol was losing interest and the hairdressers were often quiet. Strathaven is just a small town but it had fourteen hairdressers. I had always felt Carol would make an amazing carer as she had such a compassionate heart. She decided to quit in 2007 and Jim and I had the option to either leave or take over the whole shop (Carol went on to train as a nurse). The landlord wouldn't let us stay in just the small part. I remember feeling deja vu and fearful of the extra expense and responsibility. Jim could see a way of expanding and having a little art gallery that supported local artists and had sculptures and specialist new age greeting cards. Carol's massage and treatment room could also become a healing room which we would let out and also use if we wished to do shamanic healing. For it to work we would need rent from the healing room but so many people had expressed an interest in having a room with us if we ever had space that we didn't think it would be an issue. We took over the full premises and began working all hours to make it work. My girls were older and doing well in their education. They loved our home and their friends. It was an exciting time.

But only one Reiki therapist came forward to rent the healing room and that was only two days a week. She lasted a month and had very few clients. It seems people wanted either Jim or me so we started to diversify and he did some healing and ran development circles while I did shamanic healing as well as my readings which were still as popular as ever. As the year wore on we became more and more tired. When Jim was doing healing/ teaching work I was on the front desk and when I was doing readings, he was on the front desk. We were exhausted and our relationship was becoming tense. Also the larger premises was simply not paying its way no matter what we did. We worked so hard but were continually hit with bills out of left field. I started to feel quite ill in the run up to autumn 2008. I had constant headaches and wasn't sleeping well. My younger daughter seemed to be having a lot of anxiety at school and frequently needed to come home because of feeling sick. We now know this was IBS caused by anxiety attacks. Jim seemed to be grumpier and he didn't like cancelling clients when I was ill. He looked after my diary and it was hard to cancel someone and not be able to fit them in for four months. In October 2008 I went into the shop even though I felt ill. By the time I sat at my desk I knew I was in no state to do readings so I said to Jim that I was going home. I walked out of Blessed Bee and I never went back. I was diagnosed with uncontrolled high blood pressure which was a shock because my BP had mainly been on the low side. The headaches were coming from this and I was warned to slow down and rest or something bad would happen. Jim cancelled my clients for a month and we sadly realised that Blessed Bee had gone as far as we could take it. It had taken our health and was affecting our happiness. We were lucky that someone was ready to take over the whole lease and Jim contacted our crafts people to give them their work back and thank them. I felt raw and very ill. Jim felt that his dream was over. We had five years where we made a difference but it still hurt that, like Hamilton Psychic Forum, it had ended. In a few months I started reading from home again without the pressure of a shop. This freedom felt good.

So many good new age and spiritual shops open, thrive for a while, and then have to close. Two have closed this year that were known and respected for what they provided. They had room for clairvoyant readings and workshops and lovely stock to sell. Yet it still wasn't enough.

A good friend Toby helped Jim open a Blessed Bee website where he could sell his incenses and left over stock. I moved on but Jim found it harder. I never doubted his love but wondered sometimes if he ever regretted leaving so much behind him in Ireland for me and a dream that had gone sour for him.

.

INTERLUDE

BEING AN AUTHOR

I have always written, whether it be short stories, poems, teenage love letters to pop stars or articles for the school magazine. Writing has always given me great pleasure. I have a need to be creative. My big brother Robert was a commercial artist so he had first dibs at drawing and painting and he was amazing. My art was more, 'matchstalk men and matchstalk cats and dogs'. His was dynamic and modern. He could draw or design anything and I was very proud of his work. It seemed that I was taking after my mum who loved to write and who regularly received the odd five pound cheque for comments in the Sunday Post or Evening Times newspapers. My mum always had at least one book on the go and adored reading and words. One of our mum/daughter delights was waiting on the monthly Reader's Digest Magazine to arrive so we could enjoy the column that gave us twenty new words each month. Language bonded us.

When I was at secondary school my English teacher assumed that I would go to University to study English and was horrified when I applied for science instead. I felt I had let her down in some way but years later was able to give her an acknowledgment in one of my books. I continued to write in notebooks even as a pharmacist but felt it wasn't very good. It was mainly for me. Writing, first and foremost, relieves stress for me. It takes me away from the day to day world and into my imagination. I come back feeling revived and renewed. I wrote lot of things while I was in my early days as a professional clairvoyant. One of the successful projects was a Tarot course written from a practical and down to earth perspective. I was proud of this course and of the students who joined me whether in class or online. It was this course which would be the catalyst of me becoming a published author.

I was approaching my 50th birthday in 2011 and quite looking forward to it. I felt that spiritually and emotionally I was in a good place and that I was doing what I wanted. As usual, I was using my tarot cards for personal development after a meditation when I decided to really ask myself what was missing in my life. Was there anything that I felt I hadn't achieved or that was still a wish for me personally? Not about children or my husband, simply me. I didn't even have to turn a card as two answers came out immediately. One was that I missed having a dog. The second was that I wanted to be a published author and spend some of my time writing professionally in the years ahead. I checked my cards to ask if either or both were potentials and I got a very big yes! As far as the dog was concerned I was assured that my dog would come to me. I was happy with this. The writing aspect though showed that some magick would help and I would need to be prepared for much hard work once it had worked.

I had four weeks to go before my big birthday so I looked at the work I already had. I had some short stories and a few chapters of my first go at memoirs. I had part of a past life novel that had been in a drawer for over ten years. All of which could be potentials but I decided to focus on the memoirs and see what would happen. Then I set to work doing the magick! I decided that I would make the intent simply about being an author who was paid for her work and had a decent publishing deal. I was aware how magick can go wrong and didn't want to move professions completely; I loved my clairvoyant readings and felt I was still improving and learning. I decided to use my Rohrig tarot deck for the intent. I took out the cards that represent science, clairvoyance and writing/communication. I wanted to honour all of my occupations and skills. I was still a non-practicing pharmacist and wanted to continue as that. I was happy as a clairvoyant and didn't want to destroy that for a writing contract. So I placed the science card first, with the clairvoyant card slightly on top to the right. Then I slid the writing card under the clairvoyant card so that the clairvoyant card was still the main focus of the three cards. Rohrig tarot was off the market but I knew that sacrificing the whole deck for the intent would be worth it even though it left me with only one complete deck to work with. I mounted the card intent in a photo frame to give it stability and made it the main part of my spell/intent. I worked with it that day running my eyes over the flow of it and saying my prayers and willing it into being. It was an amazing day. I felt that, with the devotions, the offerings and the focus, that it was a good one and it would manifest.

Within a week I was contacted by a Facebook friend who had a book out saying that her publishing company was looking for Mind Body Soul authors particularly for divination. She passed me the contact email and off I went. After an initial exchange I decided to send them my sample chapters of memoirs. It was returned to me pretty quickly as they didn't do memoir type books at that time. I was so disappointed but then they asked if I had anything on the Tarot which I was known for due to columns and magazine articles. I said I had a tarot course but it was written as a course and was not formatted as a book. They asked to see it and came back with the offer of a contract if I would make it into a book. I had a contract signed and sealed five days before my fiftieth birthday and was walking on air. My tarot course which had been accessed by a few was now going to be accessed by many. I felt so happy. I would be a published author! I remember my husband telling folk at my birthday party and I felt proud and fulfilled. I only had to rewrite the damn thing now!

Transferring a modular course into a book was quite tough but I enjoyed every minute of it. John Hunt Publishing were amazing to work with. They allowed me to suggest a cover and also to feel part of the process. The proofing and copy-editing process intrigued me as did the marketing and sales. John Hunt allowed access to all areas of the process which was unheard of in publishing at that time. My first book 'Tarot Novice to Pro In One Book' was published in November 2011. I had a launch party at a local yoga studio and it was packed out. I remember being so nervous but it truly was a wonderful day. One of the thrills of my life was holding my book in my hands for the first time. I had a wee cry. I knew my mum would be very proud of me in spirit. My tarot book still sells six years later and I am still as proud of it today as I was in 2011. It was the catalyst to all my other books.

I was going through the menopause and had decided to do it completely naturally. As a pharmacist I knew both the benefits and concerns of HRT and didn't want to have chemicals in my body if I didn't need them. I was really curious to see how my body would be by simply letting nature take its course so I decided to also avoid herbs and supplements. I would use mantras and meditations instead. Sounds bonkers? Sometimes I felt bonkers but I felt committed to it. I was moving towards being a spiritual grandmother and wanted to set an example of how to have a natural and spiritual menopause journey. It struck me…what a great title for a book: 'Menopause: A Natural and Spiritual Journey'! I approached my publisher with the idea and a few of my hastily written chapters and the reader reports came back favourable. I had another book contract! This menopause book was written from my heart. It was totally honest about certain taboo things like lack of libido and chin hair and was written with compassion and understanding. The response when it came out was amazing. I had so many people thank me and such good reviews. It enabled me to write a few magazine pieces on natural menopause and get the message out there. Again, my menopause book still sells and is something I am so proud of.

Next came 'Weegie Tarot: Life of a Foolish Man'. This was my attempt to take the Major Arcana archetypes of the Tarot and rebirth them in Glasgow. The Fool would be Glaswegian - a Weegie! This book totally took over my life. So much of it was based on some of my own experiences and the main character Eddie Reilly became so dear to me that I cried when the book was finished. So did many others. This book received the most acclaim of any of my books. Tarot professionals loved it and ordinary people read it simply as a story of one man's journey through a life of poverty and sectarianism, love and loss. One of my clients saw someone reading it on a Glasgow bus and laughing out loud. An American man thought Eddie was real and that I had interviewed him for the book. This was a major compliment to me. I had invested so much of my knowledge of the tarot and real life into this book that I was bewildered when sales failed barely months after it had been published. It had been accepted into the prestigious Mitchell Library in Glasgow as an example of Glasgow Life. How could it be failing?

I did everything I could to get it moving but the arts and writing scene in Scotland seemed to favour crime fiction or Scots poetry and known names. 'Weegie Tarot'? What? The title was a problem in the USA where the book had flat-lined early on. People thought it was about Ouija boards and didn't buy. I was heartbroken. The book was selling more in Australia than at home due to ex pats and even those sales dried up. My publisher John Hunt admitted that he felt the company was 'too London-centric' for such a Scottish book. They didn't have the contacts in Scotland or the influence. I had to accept that the book that I had become most connected with and that had the best reviews ever, was dead in the water.

I put that behind me and wrote a few more MBS books which did okay. 'Maybe The Universe Just Isn't That Into You!' was my send up of the New Age movement and all the pretensions I saw every day. I felt able to risk this because I was part of the movement and felt it was being taken over by fluffy bunny rainbow unicorn types or even worse, con artists. This wee book was written in a rage in one week and again, it got me a contract. 'How to Read an Egg' was my mad divination book that had come out of finding out that my granny on my dad's side had been a clairvoyant in Glasgow who read eggs. I wondered if I could do this too and after a hilarious attempt decided to see what other old/weird/nonsensical form of divination I could fail at. I enjoyed buttock reading, tea leaf reading and learning about all sorts of 'mancys' i.e. bibliomancy etc. This was a kind of teaching book that allowed people to try these old or weird forms of divination with me. It was written with humour and I must admit I had so much fun writing it. I used volunteers from my Facebook page. We had a brilliant time. 'How to Read an Egg' still sells but much more in the USA than here. This made me even more disappointed in 'Weegie Tarot' as I felt it could have done so much better. It was stuck in a non-fiction category when it was becoming obvious that most folk had read it simply for the story rather than as a tarot book.

By 2014 I was ready to try some fiction writing. I decided to really go out of my comfort zone. I still knew I wanted to write something with a spiritual or clairvoyant angle and it may as well be set in Glasgow as that is what I knew. So I asked myself - what is a genre I don't read and don't really like? The answer was crime fiction so I decided that would be my next writing genre! I always try to stretch myself and boy, would this stretch me. I work with titles first! I feel once I have a great title I can move forward and let it encapsulate the tone of the book. So I normally go to sleep on it and let lots of potentials slip around my head. It came to me very suddenly: 'Fortune Killer'! This would be a play on that denigrating phrase 'fortune teller' and my main character would be a clairvoyant serial killer with a big list! She would be a disgruntled woman past her heyday and on the way out after rumours of fixing a live mediumship show. She would be funny and know magick. In fact...could she kill her victims with magick? Tick! Yes! And from there it flowed until Faith Hope was a fully engaging character with a back story to match and the joy of two unusual Spirit Guides, Johnny Cash and Fred Astaire. I was on fire with this. I gave full rein to my humour and let it be as dark as it needed. Every day writing was a pleasure like no other. My Beta readers loved it but indicated that they would never want to get on my bad side! I was still doing readings and my health was suffering but 'Fortune Killer' allowed me to just have fun. I decided to try and self-publish it via Amazon as I felt it was again very Scottish and that I would be better taking on the marketing etc. myself for it. Self-publishing was quite hard although I had help from Mark Wilson, a tremendous Indie author who already had self-published a few of his own books. I enjoyed designing my own cover which was quite eye catching and enjoyed all of the other processes but formatting for kindle and paperback etc. just was too much. Mark actually stepped in and rescued me when I was about to throw in the towel. Before I knew it 'Fortune Killer' was out and the reviews were good. I felt exhausted, truly spent and I knew it would be a wee while before I wrote any fiction again.

However, when I get an idea for a book, it refuses to go away. A few weeks after 'Fortune Killer' was released I decided to write love story set in a pharmacy! Again, I had started with a title first then the ins and outs of the book flowed. 'The Prescription' would be about how every prescription tells a story and not all stories have happy endings. I had enjoyed nearly twenty years of a pharmacy career and knew that pharmacies could be very funny, sad and even vulgar places. You need to have a sense of humour to be a pharmacist and a strong stomach. I knew some of the stories would make folk laugh and cry. The characters of Gerry and Danny came very easily and I grew to love Danny. But this book left me in tears many times too. I had to do quite a bit of research into pancreatic cancer and I simply couldn't believe how much of a death sentence this form of cancer could be. I knew that the book could help raise awareness and wanted to get it so right. I believe my character's experiences were accurate and sympathetic. Once again I self-published with the help of Mark and his formatting skills. My younger daughter Jill has always been exceptional at English and was my proofreader and copy-editor for both my fiction books. So I now have an in house copy-editor and don't need to badger Mark to format for me anymore.

I wanted to go back and do some more MBS so I did a short book on love which was only put out on kindle. Again, Jill copy-edited and formatted and a little idea started to crystallise in my mind. I enjoyed self-publishing as it meant that the time from finishing writing to actually publishing was short. I also enjoyed the fact that royalties are paid monthly whereas traditional publishes pay twice a year. I was so grateful to John Hunt Publishing for my start and for all the experience they had given me but I felt I wanted more. I wanted to have all parts of my books controlled by me and most of royalties come directly to me. So I decided to start my own small publishing company. This would firstly publish my own and maybe some of Jill's books but our expertise could also be used for people who wanted to self-publish but didn't have the time or skills to do so. Saraswati Creative Publishing was born. There is lot to do and learn before we offer services to others but I know we will in the future.

The one niggle and disappointment that was in the back of my head was how poorly 'Weegie Tarot' had performed. There was interest in making it into a play but this had stalled and I felt that some of my best work was simply dead in the water. I decided to ask to buy my rights back from John Hunt Publishing. There was clause in my contract that if a book has seriously under performed for three years and if agreement could be made by both parties, then rights could be transferred. 'Weegie' fitted the bill and in 2016 I bought my rights back. I changed the title to 'Karma City' and self-published it as Urban Fiction via Saraswati Creative Publishing on Amazon. Now it has a chance to either have wings or falter. It looks like it may have wings!

So, in six years I have written eight books! This is a dream come true for me and after these memoirs I have plans for many more. I feel strongly that Saraswati Creative Publishing will be the main course of action for most of my books. I hope it will eventually help others too. There are a lot of good writers who just don't know where to start and those who have maybe been rejected by mainstream publishers but still would like to self-publish but need help with proofing, copy-editing, formatting and marketing. There are people with stories to tell to a niche audience, people who simply want a family book published. And hopefully disabled people, people with mental health issues, dyslexics and people on the Autism spectrum who all have stories or advice that wouldn't be in a form accepted by a traditional publisher. We want to help people find their words!

Writing is like breathing to me. It simply is part of what I do. I couldn't live without it and am grateful to have been given two talents in this life, as a clairvoyant and also as a writer. I am truly blessed.

16

Working at home gave me a new lease of life. I had experienced having premises and all the hassle that comes with them and was glad to be out of it. Now it could be simply about the readings, teachings and giving more time to my spiritual practices. I have always meditated at least for half an hour each day but on work days that was mainly to open up for my work. Now I felt I could simply meditate for me and become stronger in my spiritual discipline and devotions. I made my reading room cosy and was relieved that, once again, my clients followed me. It would be a great time of spiritual expansion for me.

One of the joys was starting to host a Moon-lodge. In tribal societies a Moon-lodge is where women go to menstruate each month. In ancient times all women were hormonally tuned into the phases of the moon. They ovulated at the full moon and menstruated at the new moon or dark moon. The Moon-lodge was not a place of shame that it became later in some cultures - some African tribes banish their menstruating women to a hut or shed which is unsanitary. Women are at their most magickal at moon time (menstruation) and this led to a fear in some patriarchal societies. So women were made to feel shame in their bodies instead of being revered for being the givers of life. In many cultures moon blood is seen as so magickal it is used in rituals. In others it is shunned and seen as dirty. But the traditional honouring Moon-lodges were a place for women to gather and look after one another for four or five days. They cleansed their bodies with herbs and oils. They plaited each other's hair and offered advice on matters of concern. Sacred sage was burned and women relaxed and simply let their blood flow. The younger girls of the tribe and the Grandmothers (those who were through moonpause) looked after the chores for the moon women while they rested and reinvigorated for another month or a pregnancy.

A modern version of this is when women gather at the new moon to nurture one another, learn from one another and relax and meditate. I hosted a Moon-lodge in my reading room and it was a mix of spiritualties: Native American, Heathen, Christian and Hindu. That one evening a month we came together for teachings, succour and friendship. There were opening and closing prayers and each month the Moon-lodge was led by a different member who would teach us something. We sat in a circle the way women have done for eternity. There is no 'head of the table' in a circle. The Moon-lodge became a happy evening every month and forged bonds that would not be broken. This was where I first heard of Goddess Durga from our Hindu women. I have so many happy memories of these nights but after a few years the women moved on with life and we eventually closed Silver Birch Moon-lodge. I am now part of a family Moon-lodge which is partly face to face and partly conducted through Facebook. I am the first spiritual Grandmother of our Moon-lodge and it has given me the confidence to walk my talk in the larger world.

My health wasn't ideal. I needed a second hearing device and I was dizzy a lot of the time. Jim's spinal arthritis was worsening and I suspected that I was beginning to show signs of a family hereditary disease called Sjogren's Syndrome. My mum and dad both had this, and both my older brothers and niece. Although seen as a disease where glands become blocked and you need eye drops and synthetic saliva, it has many other systemic problems too. My skin broke out and my hips and ankles became very sore. I had flare ups where fatigue would simply stop me in my tracks. Being at home was a life saver. Jim and I did a couple of workshops but the house wasn't ideal for them so we gave up. Jim was involved in some animal healing which he loved. Yet he didn't feel fulfilled and was becoming more distant. The energy deteriorated in our home and this led to the split in 2010. This was a very sad time and we all look back on it as something that hurt us all and that we would not allow to happen again.

My readings became longer and I felt, even more in depth. It was hard to shut off from them and my meditations were taking longer and longer. I felt it was worth it because of the depth I was going to but there is always pay off for this and with me it was exhaustion and pain. I was picking up more and more. In one reading I had the most awful feeling of something steel being drawn across the middle of my body like I had been cut in two. I felt dizzy with the pain, so much so that the client looked very worried. I explained that I felt I had the spirit of her husband and that he wanted to talk to her but that I felt this awful trauma around my middle. She said, 'Yes that's my husband all right and I don't want to talk to him. He threw himself under a train!'

On another occasion I was reading for a woman and tuned into her mother who was alive. I felt the most horrible searing pain in my legs, like my veins had been ripped out. I told her and she gasped. She said that her mother was in hospital going through an operation to strip her varicose veins out of her legs at that particular time. I had felt it even though she had an anaesthetic! I tended to be able to feel where people were hurting and would point to their shoulder or their back and was right. I could also see a rough red colour in the aura that showed me where there was damage or inflammation. This came in handy for reminding women to go for their smears if I saw what a believed was inflamed cells in their cervix. Having a background knowledge of anatomy from my pharmacy course helped a lot. I could also sometimes see when something was missing from the body as it showed as a kind of energy gap with redness around it. This allowed me to see if a woman had had a hysterectomy. Most women were fascinated that I could do this but one man who came was freaked and didn't wait for his full reading. As he sat down I saw that there was the energy gap where a testicle should have been. I asked him if he had had a testicle removed. He said yes, put his money on the table and left. I never saw him again.

I also was able to pick up on scars on people's bodies. Sometimes I did this just to show them that I was genuine in my gift. People like proof of the paranormal. I did this on Mystic Challenge where I picked up that my hidden celebrity had a scar above his left eye. It turned out to be David Emmanuel the fashion designer and he did indeed have a scar above his left eye. I discovered an interesting thing though. The redness of scarring looks exactly the same to me in the aura as a tattoo. So if the redness looked a certain shape I could tell the person about their tattoo. This was more like a party trick but was very funny and could certainly get a client's attention.

One day a man came for a reading who worked in a very rich industry. We were looking at options for jobs and he said he wanted to go to a certain place. The card that represented this was the Ten of Swords which is a bad card predicting trauma and potential disaster and hurt. I showed him it and advised him against it. He said he would still go as it was a place he could make massive career movement. I saw there and then that he would go and it would change his life. I said to him to remember that when this incident connected with the ten of swords happened that I knew he would make it home alive. I asked him to believe in it. He was shocked but agreed. I didn't see him for a few years and when he next came for a reading I didn't recognize him. He looked healthy and full of energy and totally renewed. He told me that had indeed gone to the 'Ten of Swords' country and had been involved in a kidnapping by insurgents. He was held at gunpoint and thought he would die. Then he remembered what I had said and it was true. He made it home. It changed him as a man. He renewed his priorities. This was fated to happen for him.

So my readings were intense to say the least. I knew I needed to be very disciplined to keep at this level of intuition and I took my job very seriously. I still hated being called a fortune teller and I suppose I had a little bit of an ego about my readings. I wanted to be known as one of the best. So I had to laugh when the universe handed me a big lesson. My elder daughter had passed her driving test and had a wee run-around car. Her car insurance would be less expensive if I was a named driver as I had no claims. She asked to put me on and said that I was a clairvoyant on the form. When her insurance schedule came through my job was listed as 'Circus Performer'! She thought I would be annoyed but I couldn't stop laughing. Me…a circus performer! I could hardly get up and down my own stairs.

It was around this time that I had one of my most powerful and intense past life dreams. It felt like it went on all night. I remember looking down at my hands as I lay in the sun. My skin was pale and freckled just like it was when I was child in Blairbeth but I had petticoats and boots on. I was sweating and pulled my long plaits forward and patted the frizz down. My hair was reddish gold, again like I had as a child in this life. But it was a warm sultry place and I was aware of being over the hill from my homestead where my mum was making dinner. I remember sitting up quickly as I sensed people around me. To my horror I saw three Native Americans, one of whom lifted me up and strode off into the woods while the others followed. I struggled and screamed until I saw they had knives and were looking at me with rage. The next thing I knew I was walking and had been for days. My feet were sore and my dress was ripped and I was exhausted. I was forced to eat some goo that made me feel sick but it filled me up. And then I was walking and walking again. I was heartbroken and thought of every way to escape that I could. But the more we walked the more I knew that I would be lost and eaten by wild animals. So we walked more.

Later on in the dream I was in a camp and in a big tepee with lots of people and was presented to what looked like the chief of the tribe. He had kind eyes and I felt he would look after me. Yet there was one woman with eyes of stone and she was the person who taught me how to do things. I could never do anything right and she beat me a lot. Then the dream switched to gatherings where I was more part of it and sitting near the chief. I liked his laugh and his kindly eyes. I wanted him to love me like he loved the others. I had started to understand the language and knew who was clever and who was silly. I could barely remember my family now. They had never caught up and rescued me. I had believed that for so long but now I didn't. The last thing I remember as I woke up was approaching the chief as he lay down to sleep. I was on my knees and in my head I asked for his love. I wanted to be his family. He opened his kind eyes and I said to him, 'I am no longer Mary Campbell.'

When I woke up I was very confused as to where I was but Jim was sleeping softly with me in bed and the dawn was breaking. I felt exhausted and knew that this was an important dream. I got a coffee and stared to think on it. I have been aware of Native American past lives but this was the first one that I woke from with a name. When Jim came down I told him the dream and said my name was Mary Campbell. He said it was common name but why not try and Google it and see what comes up. What happened next floored me. The Google search showed up a story of a child called Mary Campbell who was one of the last white children stolen by natives in the USA. She was taken and forced to walk hundreds of miles to be gifted to a Delaware chief whose granddaughter had died. Then the tribe was displaced by the government to Ohio where they had a small partition of land near a river. Mary Campbell eventually forgot about her birth family and became an important member of the tribe. She was gifted her moccasins and there is even a children's book called The Beaded Moccasins that is a fictional account of her life. There is a Mary Campbell cave in Ohio. I read all this with a lump in my throat and total awe. The drawing of her on the book was so like me as a child in this life - red hair, freckles and blue eyes. I cried my eyes out as I read that after a few years her birth family found her and took her back to her old ways. This was a wrench away from her new family, her new spirituality and her new sense of being. I couldn't stop crying for myself. Because I knew that I was and had been Mary Campbell.

Another dream that seemed to be haunting me was one of a wee girl Cavalier King Charles spaniel who I knew was waiting for us and needed us. She seemed to be calling out to me in my dream and I knew she was called Lottie. This became such an intense feeling that I searched adverts and Dogs Trust for her. As we headed to the end of 2011 I knew that she was calling me and needed me to find her. The day before New Year's Eve we had a call from a Cavalier rescue society to say they had a wee girl in need of a home. She had been rescued from a puppy farm in England. She was only about six but had had about ten litters of pups. They were going to kill her as she was worn out and done but the rescuers took her. They showed me a photo of her and I knew it was my Lottie. Jim and I picked her up. She had the sweetest, kindest face and immediately came and sat by Jim and me. The rescuers thought she was going into heat again as there was a little blood flow. We brought her home and the girls started giving her all the love she had never had. She had a very swollen belly and we knew she would need the vet in the New Year. We had been told that she had forgotten how to bark as she had never been responded to in the puppy farm. She had lived outside in a cold kennel and all she did was have pups and then have them taken away. Her eyes were so sad. Yet she trusted us. She loved her treats and sitting on the couch with us all. My wee girl had found me.

She had so many cuddles and good food. I was convinced she was in heat because of little blood stains. Later on at night she barked at the TV at Edward Scissorhands of all things. We let out a big yell of congratulations! I had made up a bed in my reading room but was a wee bit concerned that she was bleeding a wee bit more heavily than normal heat. But she had a very overworked womb so I felt we would just see how it went. She also seemed to be having difficulty walking. She looked far older than six years old. We had more fun with her until bed time. Jill decided to sleep on the floor with her as she couldn't bear to leave her. When I checked on them both early next morning, Jill had stayed awake cuddling Lottie and reassuring her all night. There was too much blood for my liking. Something was badly wrong. I had to carry her out for a pee and she looked so sweet but so done in. In just twenty-four hours Lottie had entered our hearts and found a deep place there. We loved her so much. I called the vet and was given an appointment right away. Jill carried her in a blanket and my heart was doing somersaults. It was New Year's Eve or Hogmanay in Scotland. The vet checked her out and sadly said that poor Lottie had gone into shock and was dying. Her womb had basically perforated and she was bleeding internally too. I had thought maybe she would get medication and we could take her home to bring in the Bells with us as our new family member. It was not to be. The vet allowed us to say our sad goodbyes. Lottie looked at me with what I felt was gratitude. And then she was gone. I paid for her injections and her cremation and we went home broken. How could we have loved her so much? She is still deep in all our hearts even today. I see her spirit around but it still hurts knowing she was calling me and yet she only had one day with us. Jill says it was the best day of Lottie's life and I am glad she had it with us. We will never regret it. But how can people treat animals like that? How can puppy farms get away with it? It breaks my heart. We didn't celebrate the New Year that night.

As we moved into 2013 I was aware that both Jim and I were struggling with the stairs in our home. Jill had moved out to go to university and Jennifer would be moving into her own flat soon as she had a good teaching job. The garden was becoming too much for us and new school was being built right at the back of our home. Trees had been cut down and we were looking onto a playing field. It was noisy and we had very little privacy. It was time to be moving on again and once again hope that my enduring clients would follow me.

17

I sat down to write this last chapter with a grin on my face. Over 60,000 words and nearly there! I felt tired though, so decided to have a wee nap before I started. During the nap I had a spirit visit me and it was very pleasant. She came to say that her story should be in the book because it would make people happy, and she was right! So here it is. I had a lovely friend called Mhairi who was the kind of woman you had to watch what you said around her. If she had something and you said you liked it she would simply give you it; that's how kind she was! So I learned never to really say I liked either her perfume or an ornament. Mhairi was very creative and enjoyed making banners for Blessed Bee. She loved her readings with me especially as her mum used to come through from spirit. Her mum was her best friend and she missed her so very much. Mhairi was simply a joy to be around but she was always on the go and I had warned her many times about slowing down. She had high blood pressure and sometimes I worried when I saw her cards. I was always telling her to relax as were her doctors.

One day as I was finishing up my readings in Blessed Bee, Jim came in and closed the door. He told me that Mhairi had died that morning of a heart attack. It was such an impossible thought that I actually asked him, 'Mhairi who?' not taking in that it could possibly be my friend. The part of Mhairi's story that is inspiring is actually around her death. She collapsed and her husband held her as she faded. She told him she loved him and then she looked right over his shoulder, smiled and said one word, 'Mum!' Then she died. I know this will give so much comfort to those of you who have lost a parent. Mhairi loved her mum so much and at the end it was her mum who came to take her home.

Jim and I moved to a wee cottage in the lovely countryside in 2013. It had fields on three sides and you needed to come along a winding single track road to get to it. I hoped my clients would follow me but knew if they didn't it was still the right home for us. It was so pretty and good for the soul. There were a few clients that nearly ended up in Ayr by missing the cottage turnoff and we needed to print out a map and instructions to get here. I stopped working so much at night as the lanes were truly a wee bit spooky and if I was a lone female client I would have turned back. But still they came. We ran a couple of workshops as well and the fresh air and natural setting was very conducive to spirituality. It was and is such a lovely place to live.

It was nice to know that I lost very few clients with the move. I was reading for one of my lovely business clients and he thanked me for advice that had had saved him a lot of money when I saw an investment was not good. He said he was relieved he had moved it and also said that some of his colleagues were impressed too. I said I didn't think his was the type of occupation that many people would own up to seeing a clairvoyant. He told me that I wasn't his clairvoyant - I was his future trends strategist! Now that is a name I like!

The first winter in the cottage was hell because we underestimated how costly the oil central heating would be. I was so used to having direct debits that I wasn't used to buying bulk oil for our tank. We learned to enjoy wearing lots of layers. Rain flooded the lanes and left us cut off. This meant that sometimes clients simply couldn't get through. I decided that at some point I would try to do some Skype readings so clients wouldn't need to be disappointed if rain or ice held them back from coming. But things were changing with my health. I had a couple of sores on my legs which turned into leg ulcers which became infected. The first three months of 2014 were spent having my legs washed and dressed by nurses twice a week and then compression therapy applied. This was one of the sorest things I have had done to me. I also had to promise to elevate my legs in bed for most of the day. I found this incredibly sore and boring. I tried meditating as much as I could but when the understanding came that spirit was actively slowing me down, I would put it out of my mind. I had always worked hard and had many more years in me.

One of the joys of 2014 is that we were gifted the most beautiful wee dog, a Lhasa Apso called Benji. He was such a handsome boy, cute but very stubborn. He stole my heart right away and Jim soon followed. I finally had my longed for dog. I was a bit confused because I felt I would have a wee girl but Benji just became my best companion. He would sit beside me in bed when I was ill. He would bat away my phone if I wasn't paying attention to him. When he had his little bad dreams my heart just melted. I will always be thankful to Andrea for such a wonderful gift. Benji is one of the most loved dogs ever. He even has his own YouTube video where he is chased by a spirit dog! He is a star.

My Sjogren's disease was worsening and the pain and exhaustion was intense but I still fought it. I had books to write, clients to see and a life to lead. My Grandmother role was becoming very important to me. I felt I needed to pass on teachings and lessons and felt that I would do this through my books. I was also informally mentoring two young women who were very clairvoyant and who I knew were the next generation of talented tarot readers. I even called one 'Mini Me' because she had the same way of looking at things and adored the Rohrig deck. I also began my devotions to Durga with more discipline and worked with The Medicine Wheel every day. Yet some days I simply found it too sore to wash and dress. There was more trauma to come.

My husband Jim was becoming more and more stiff and sore due to spinal arthritis but I also realised that he was forgetting things and becoming frustrated by it. I persuaded him to go to the doctor and very soon he was seeing consultants and being sent for all sorts of scans in case he had a brain tumour. I was so very worried, far more worried than he was, although maybe he was just good at not showing it. The result showed that he had a cyst in his frontal lobe that was disrupting the flow of information to the memory part of his brain. There was nothing that could be done as the cyst was embedded into his skull and would have been too dangerous to move. He would just have to live with it and hope it didn't move or calcify more. So the results were better than they could have been but it meant that Jim had to also come

149

to terms that there were things that he simply couldn't do now. Jim's diagnosis shook me up. I felt that I didn't want so many people coming to our cottage for readings so I cut back a lot and did more on the internet. But by April 2015 the health of both of us had deteriorated and I decided to do my readings only remotely either by Skype or Mp3. Spirit was slowing us down but I was still lagging behind.

In the midst of all this my dad visited me in a dream. It was such an amazing lucid dream. I will remember it always. My dad often communicates through dreams. In the dream we were looking out at the view of North Berwick, a place where we used to have holidays. I remember saying that it would be perfect if Mum were here and he indicated she was and pointed to cafe on top of a hill where she was sitting reading, her favourite thing in the world. I was happy that she was with us but dad urged me to look at the view. He pointed to the two bays split by the harbour which had lots of little boats bobbing up and down peacefully. Then he pointed out sea and I could see a large wave like a tsunami coming towards the shore. It was traveling fast. It hit the first bay and wrecked all the little boats and I remember feeling so sad and also worried that the other bay, that had a children's paddling pool in it, would be decimated too. But he showed me that the harbour wall and the rocks had absorbed the wave and the second bay was still calm and safe. Then he nodded as though to say 'understand' which I didn't. Then I woke up.

I was worried because I know that water in a dream means emotions and here my dad had shown me a big wave of emotion coming towards the shore that had wrecked everything in its path. Yet he had also showed me that one bay was still safe and calm and untouched. I resolved to wait and see but prepared myself for this emotional tsunami by getting ahead with work. It hit two days later when an incident happened to my nephew that was so intensely unfair that it made the news and eventually the law was changed because of it. I was so worried but felt that he would find safe harbour where it was calm, as my dad had suggested in the dream. Yet I felt there was a lesson still to hit as I couldn't really pinpoint what the wrecked boats meant. The next day I opened the newspaper only to see that a large wave had hit the bays of North Berwick and wrecked all the boats in the harbour! My dad had not just shown me a metaphysical meaning in the dream

150

but had directly shown me what was going to happen to his beloved harbour. And to think he used to hate all this 'spooky' stuff.

2015 turned into one of the most upsetting years as not only was I in a lot of pain and Jim deteriorating but my younger daughter was diagnosed with a severe form of Obsessive Compulsive Disorder called Pure O. This form of the illness is about terrifying thoughts going round and round the persons mind and the compulsions they use to try to keep them at bay. It is debilitating for the person and almost unbearable for a parent to watch a child dealing with it. Some days it would keep her from going over the doorstep. Others it would tire her out so much that she was exhausted. On the surface Jill could look okay yet be suffering so much inside. She could be happy and be having fun only for a random obsession to kick in and pull her to the edge of reason. These obsessions can be so far away from the person's day to day normality that it is shocking. At one point Jill would carry a bottle of water in her hand when she went out (the compulsion) as she was sure she would be the victim of an acid attack (the obsession).

It took a long time for her diagnosis due to the paltry state of NHS mental health services. It seemed almost unfair that an oldie like Jim was receiving care for his brain problem far more quickly than a young adult. Jill had good support systems, her family, her boyfriend and her friends and some good alternative therapists but other children and young adults don't. Anyone on my Facebook page that post silly memes about 'being a little bit OCD' or quizzes to see 'How OCD are you?' are quickly put right by me as to what a debilitating and even life threatening condition it can be. I have a bee in my bonnet and I wouldn't wish this mental health condition on my worst enemy. My young daughter is one of the bravest and strongest people I know. Before she can apply herself to anything each day she has to fight simply to control her mind. It can be exhausting for me watching her - she has to actually live with it. Luckily with therapy and mindfulness and support, things are improving. Jill is writing a book about her experiences which I feel will be a hard read for me as her mum but will totally help so many young people with the condition.

By 2016 I was only doing readings on Skype. I was slowing down but not maybe as fast as I could. I am a stubborn Taurus and am also used to thinking I am superwoman. My daughters say I am a workaholic. I was still writing my books and really enjoying it. Words come easy to me and it is a joy when it all flows. When I was too sore to do Skype readings I would write instead of resting. I wore two hearing devices and had adapted headphones so Skype was okay as long as the connection showed me the person's face. Over the course of the winter my hearing deteriorated and I was diagnosed with arthritis in my wrists and neck as well as Sjogren's. Spirit was giving me lessons and for once I decided to listen. In April 2017 I retired from clairvoyant readings. I had to admit defeat with my own health and also knew that I wanted to spend as much time with Jim and my family and friends as I could. I felt I had missed out. I had worked since I was twelve and had a Saturday job with my mum. I never took much maternity leave with either of my girls. I had inherited my Dad's work ethic and it actually had backfired on me. I had gone from being a successful pharmacist, to a successful clairvoyant to a successful author; all the while putting myself last. I was sick. I needed time to repair myself and simply be. Jim also had a prostate scare which once again floored me and also ongoing brain tests. Telling my lovely loyal clients that I was retiring was one of the hardest things I have ever done. I cried a lot. I knew I would miss so many of them but I knew I had made the right decision. It was all very synergetic anyway. The two young women who I had been so delighted with in their progression in their spiritual paths each took the plunge and became professional clairvoyants. The baton was being passed on and I couldn't think of two better young women to carry it forward for their generation. Susan and Mechelle know that I will be there any time they need me and will always have their backs.

The summer of 2017 was a very special time. I rested as much as I could and enjoyed seeing friends and family. My elder daughter was married and it was such a happy day. I wrote parts of this book but only when I felt I was well enough. Now we are in autumn and I am ready to begin my new phase properly. You see I may have retired from readings but I am still a clairvoyant and spiritual Grandmother. There is much for me to do and I have a new wee friend to help me. Her name is Nelly and she is a Chinese Crested Powder-puff dog. She was another gift from Spirit and is nervous, silly, funny, determined and is my shadow. Benji needed a wee pal as we felt he was a bit bored at times. We can't take him for long walks due to our mobility issues so he plays a lot in the garden. Now he has a wee girlfriend to hang about with.

Two years ago when I was struggling with my readings and the work surrounding them such as typing up rituals or spiritual advice and goals for clients, my daughter suggested I start a YouTube channel. This would mean that I could make a video of say, how to smudge your home, and load it up and then refer people to it rather than individually type it up and send it to them. I had enjoyed YouTube for a few years as a viewer and thought it would be a good idea but was nervous. But I found that I enjoyed it. I have done so much television and being in front of a camera wasn't a problem for me. Two years on and I am heading for 1000 subscribers with over 60,000 views! I have advice videos up on tarot, magick, healing and all things spiritual. The Colette Clairvoyant channel has become a little community of like-minded souls and so many of my old clients have joined me and we continue to chat and learn from one another. I don't make money from it (that was never the reason for doing it) but I do feel it helps my book sales which is always a bonus. I have plans to do live streams and connect even further. My hearing doesn't interfere with this and I only make videos when I feel well enough. I feel I am becoming the spiritual Grandmother both in books and on social media. Long may it continue as it is a joy to me. I also have plans for Saraswati Creative Publishing. I intend to publish my own books via this resource but hope it will help others to have their work published too. It is very exciting.

But there is something even more important for me to do spiritually which follows on from a very amazing journey with White Storm a few years ago. That night he asked me to go into a very deep meditation. He wished to show me his true, pure form and said I would need to trust him as I would be in awe with what he showed but he would bring me back and would give me time before we ever journeyed so far again. I agreed although I was apprehensive. I have trusted him all my life and I know he has my best interests at heart. I prepared my meditation well and after much time he came and summoned me. I took his hand and in a bright flash I was traveling very, very fast upwards through a white haze of light like a snowstorm of tiny snowflakes. I knew I had left my body but when I looked at my beloved White Storm he was the most beautiful spiral of icy white light. His spiral was spinning at a speed I can't explain with words. It spun so fast it was like just a vibration of pure white light. And then I realised that I too was the same. At that point I nearly flew back into my body but I felt energetically connected to the energy that was/is White Storm. He guided me into circle with five other beings of light. And when we connected making a circle of seven, that circle began to spin and vibrate and become a pure vibration of light too. It felt like we were only one of many spinning circles of light all connected. I have never felt such joy or bliss. And then we were back in my room. I had a terrible headache and White Storm was back to being the Native American guide that I know and love.

I looked at him and said, 'So that was the real you? Why haven't you shown me this before?' and he answered, 'At what time in your life do you think you would have been ready to see me as I truly am? When you were a child? It would have terrified you! At a time before you had the knowledge and discipline you have now? No. That wouldn't have been good. You know I have had many, many lives on earth. You understood that. You were in some of them. So you were always going to be familiar and at peace with this form of me, this Native American. But it is a cloak. I could have chosen from many of my past life forms but this one was always the one you would be understanding of. But now you have seen me truly.' And he left me to let it all sink in.

Part of me felt slightly betrayed and part of me felt so bloody stupid for not actually sussing this out. But I have always said that I never, ever searched too deeply into the Great Mystery because it is meant to be a great mystery! I have no need to go mad, thinking on things too much that would hurt my brain. Plus I have always been too busy doing readings and running workshops! But now? Well now I feel I have the time and I am inquisitive. I am looking forward to doing all my spiritual Grandmother projects, YouTube, writing my books, helping others walk their talk as well as simply enjoying being human. But I am really excited about the journeys to come with White Storm. Who knows...maybe that will be Memoirs of a Clairvoyant Volume 2?

Many Blessings,

Colette

.

ACKNOWLEDGEMENTS

How can you acknowledge everyone in a span of 56 years? I have to say a big thank you to everyone who has ever connected with me because you have made me who I am today. That must also include spirits and guides. My never-ending thanks particularly go to White Storm who has taught me and shaped me and seems ready to continue his journey with me. I am truly blessed.

I would like to thank my clients who have made my working life a delight. Every single one of you is precious to me. To those who became friends and others who allowed me to be a mentoring force in their lives - I can't thank you enough.

To my copy-editor Jillian Halket and my cover designer Christopher Smith, thank you for your work in making this book a reality.

To my birth family and my spiritual family - thank you for the huge influence you have had on my life.

To Sooz, Donna Marie, Alison, Karen, Chris, Hazel, Lesley, Andrea, Susan, Mechelle, Becca, Lauren, and all the women that have connected with me spiritually. I love and admire you all.

To Jim. My darling husband: what can I say? Simply, I love you and the best is yet to come.

And to my two daughters Jennifer and Jill. My reason for being. Having you both has been the best thing I have ever done and I love and admire you both. Strong, compassionate young women who will pass their values on to the next generation. You both are stars!

To Amma. Your compassion inspires me every day. How I long for a hug!

And finally, to Durga. Namaste! Thank you Goddess for all my blessings received.

ABOUT THE AUTHOR

Colette Brown is a retired clairvoyant and author who lives in rural Scotland with her husband and her two beloved dogs. She enjoys her role as spiritual grandmother and teacher and her new found platform of social media including her YouTube channel Colette Clairvoyant. Colette is author of nine books, six Mind Body Soul and three novels.

Connect with her on YouTube and Facebook @Colette Clairvoyant

30042468R00095

Printed in Great Britain
by Amazon